Thetford Forest

is the largest pine forest in southern England and is entirely man-made. Its 50 000 acres were planted, from 1922, in the early days of the Forestry Commission. In general most of the forest is freely open to walkers, cyclists and horse riders using recognised paths and tracks and there is a Forest Centre near Brandon that caters for a wider range of uses of the forest as well as for walking. There are a number of species of deer and other wildlife that you may see during the walks and the forest is important for its conservation value generally, as well as for recreation and, of course, its timber production.

THE FOREST CODE

Guard against all risk of fire

Protect trees, plants and wildlife

Leave things as you find them, take nothing away

Keep dogs under control

Avoid damaging buildings, fences, hedges, walls and signs

Leave no litter

Observe all warning signs and notices

Peddars Way

Thetford Forest Walks

Twenty circular walks in and around Thetford Forest

SIMON MALONE

who spent all his working life with the Forestry Commission, starting in Hampshire and Kent in his early years, then spending twenty years in Thetford Forest, latterly as the Harvesting Manager, before retiring in March 2003

Dedicated to Aisling, my grand daughter
born in July 2000

Larks Press

Published by the Larks Press
Ordnance Farmhouse, Guist Bottom, Dereham
Norfolk NR20 5PF
01328 829207
email: Larks.Press@btinternet.com

May 2004

Printed at the Lanceni Press
Garrood Drive, Fakenham

British Library Cataloguing-in-Publication Data
A catalogue record for this book is available
from the British Library

Ordnance Survey maps covering the routes described in this booklet are
Explorer Series 1:25,000 scale
Nos. 229 'Thetford Forest in the Brecks' and 230 'Diss and Harleston
Landranger Series 1:50,000 scale
Nos. 143 'Ely and Cambridge' and 144 'Thetford, Breckland and
Surrounding Area'

Acknowledgements

Thanks are due to my former colleagues in the Forestry Commission for
their advice and encouragement. Also to Suffolk County Council,
St Edmundsbury Borough Council, West Stow Anglo-Saxon Village Trust
and English Heritage for their contributions to the accuracy of this book.

The drawings are by Robert Yaxley.

ISBN 1 904006 18 3

A Short History of Breckland and Thetford Forest

Breckland is an extensive region of some 370 square miles straddling the Norfolk-Suffolk border, characterised by light sandy soil. It has a field pattern hedged by ancient Scots pine trees not to be found elsewhere in England.

In recent centuries these light sandy soils, situated in the driest part of the entire UK, had relatively little agricultural value. Indeed, their main use was to graze sheep, though in the Middle Ages there were also extensive rabbit warrens, for rabbits were farmed for their meat and their fur.

The result of this type of land use was a landscape scarce in trees, with extensive areas virtually devoid of significant vegetation. Limited cultivation took place and what did was quite transient as farmers used up any natural fertility in the soil and moved on to 'brea' new ground. Hence 'break' became 'breck' and the famous local historian and naturalist W. G. Clarke coined the name Breckland in 1894.

Nowadays modern agriculture has tamed this inhospitable soil and, thanks largely to irrigation and the use of modern fertilisers, very valuable arable crops can be grown including carrots, parsnips, onions, lettuce, potatoes and sugar beet.

At the beginning of the 20th century, things had come to a head and agriculture was in the midst of depression. The few large estates in the area were struggling to balance their books. At the same time, the country had endured the Great War of 1914-18 and the government of the day was counting the cost to British woodlands. These had been stripped to provide timber for the war effort which had required vast quantities of timber for the coal mines and industry at home, and because the German naval blockades had prevented vital timber imports from reaching us.

Accordingly the Ackland Committee was set up to advise the government and its decision was to establish a Forestry Commission, a state forest industry, to create a reserve of timber against any future wars or catastrophes. And so the Forestry Commission came into being in 1919.

The first requirement was to buy or lease land suitable for afforestation and in the early 1920s plans were formulated to buy up many of the impoverished estates in Breckland. From these acquisitions, largely between 1922 and the early 1940s, Thetford Forest was created. It was to become the largest man-made pine forest inEngland and eventually reached its current size of around 20,000 hectares (50,000 acres) with a production of over 160,000 tonnes of timber per year.

It was quickly found that Scots and Corsican pines thrived in the dry sandy soils and they were the main species to be planted. Broadleaf belts, slow-growing and difficult to establish, were planted along roadsides to serve as firebreaks rather than for their amenity value. The forest thrived and by the Second World War was producing pit props for the war effort from early thinning of the young plantations.

Because the forest was originally planted in huge areas of similar age trees, it was at first rather uniform in appearance but, with the decision to embark on a clear felling programme of mature, log-rich crops in the late 1960s, the chance came to create diversity and this has led to the modern forest where variations in age structure have created a mosaic of landscape and conservation interest throughout. This has also meant that the age structure will soon be such that equal volumes of timber can be sustained indefinitely year in year out over the typical 50 to 60-year crop rotations. This fact is of great importance to the local wood-processing businesses that depend on much of this timber for their livelihood.

In parallel with all these developments came changes to the policies that directed the Forestry Commission. No longer was there to be a single objective of creating a strategic timber reserve. Instead, the woodlands have been opened up to the public and although timber revenues provide the main financial income for the Commission its management division, Forest Enterprise, is now charged with growing the timber taking full account of the increasing importance of Recreation, Wild Life and Heritage Conservation and with regard to the landscape qualities of this multi-purpose forest which is now truly a 'Forest for the People' in the 21st century.

Thetford Forest was granted Forest Park status in 1990.

Twenty Walks in and around Thetford Forest Park

by Simon Malone
(Forestry Commission Forester 1961–2003)

This little book will allow you to explore Thetford Forest Park and some of the adjoining countryside easily on foot.

The walks vary in length, ranging from a 2-mile walk suitable for all the family to a more strenuous 20-mile walk for the more serious hiker.

All walks start at easily recognised places where cars may be parked easily. It is wise to remove all valuable items from your car before you start for security reasons. Some of the walks incorporate public rights of way across adjoining farmland.

Please follow the Forest Code at all times and, in particular, observe warning signs. Thetford Forest is a working Forest and harvesting and other forest operations must be carried out as part of the necessary management of the Forest. In some instances large machinery is in use and, for your safety, it may be necessary to restrict access temporarily. Diversions to signposted or way-marked routes will be signed in such cases, though in the case of the walk routes in this booklet such diversions cannot always be guaranteed.

I hope you will enjoy your visits to the Forest, whatever the time of year, because the Forest is always changing.

The Walks

1 The Forest Centre at High Lodge

Grid reference for start TL 811852   Distance 4 miles

I have made this the first walk in this booklet because a visit to High Lodge is an excellent way to familiarise yourself with Thetford Forest Park and find out a little about the forest as a whole.

High Lodge is reached off the B1107 Thetford to Brandon road and is well signed from a number of main roads in the area by the familiar brown tourist signs. The entrance is via a three mile Forest Drive for which there is a toll to pay. There is spacious free car parking at the Centre, which is open throughout the year from 0900 until dusk.

High Lodge has become the focal point of Thetford Forest in recent years. First opened in 1992, the attractive Forest Centre was further expanded in 2002. The building is a magnificent oak- framed structure, clad in pine boards grown in the local forest and based on the design of a typical Suffolk barn. Inside are a spacious restaurant and cafeteria area and a shop in which you can buy all sorts of souvenirs and locally produced crafts. There are also toilet facilities and outdoor picnic tables on the patio and a large grassed area adjacent. Connected to the Forest Centre, and constructed to the same design, is a cycle hire and cycle accessories shop.

Cycling is an extremely popular activity in the forest and visitors can bring their own cycles or hire them from the cycle shop. The

1

forest is a very safe place to cycle, as there is no traffic, apart from some forestry traffic associated with the general management of the woodlands. As well as free range cycling there is a long distance 'Black Route' way-marked for more adventurous cyclists. The route described in this particular walk also makes an excellent short, family cycle ride, and cyclists and walkers can share the forest safely if each respects the other.

In the adjacent forest, a whole range of exciting features are available, some free and some for a charge. These include 'Go-Ape', a high ropes course taking you high into the lofty trees, a children's play area with slides, swings and other similar features and a ground level ropes course. Not far away is the Squirrel's Maze which is constructed in a large pine plantation with a squirrel climbing feature for children at its centre and, close by, there is also a sculpture trail with a number of other climbing facilities aimed at younger members of the family. There is also a wildlife observation hide in the locality.

Visitors can walk freely in the forest and there are also a number of colour-coded way-marked routes of varying lengths to follow.

This walk takes you on a long loop through High Lodge Warren, which is the largest single block of woodland in the Forest Park. The paths and tracks are in good condition and for much of the walk you follow the route on forest roads and grassy paths.

The Walk

With your back to the Forest Centre walk down the length of the open grassed area aiming for the far left-hand corner signed 'Squirrel's Maze'. Leave the grassy area and, on entering the trees, pick up a track and turn right, continuing to walk away from the centre. After a short distance you will reach a stony road opposite the entrance to the Squirrel's Maze. Turn left and walk straight ahead, ignoring turnings on either side.

Keep straight ahead on the hard road, which eventually becomes a grassy ride. This soon bears right but stick to it, continuing ahead and gently downhill until you reach another forest road on a bend.

Turn right onto this road and follow it uphill for a quarter of a mile until the road divides. Turn right, still on a hard road that stretches ahead of you as a long straight road for some distance.

You will pass through an area where there are old research plots on either side that contain a mixture of different tree species. You are free to explore the tracks through the plots but return to the straight hard road in due course.

Keep straight ahead on the road for about a mile and a half, ignoring all side turnings, until the road approaches a small grass field on the right. Just before you reach the field turn right down a sandy track that drops gently downhill.

Just before the track reaches the bottom of the slope there is a crossing of several tracks. Take the second track on the right and follow this as a sandy path at first downhill then climbing gently up to another crossing of tracks. On the way, notice the low twin banks stretching away to the left, which are the remains of old Warren boundaries.

At the junction of tracks take the second turning on the left, which is a sandy path, climbing gently uphill ahead of you. This eventually passes another small grass field on the left before joining an all-weather path and reaching a stony road opposite a concrete reservoir building.

Cross the road and choose any of the paths ahead, which will take you back to the Visitor Centre.

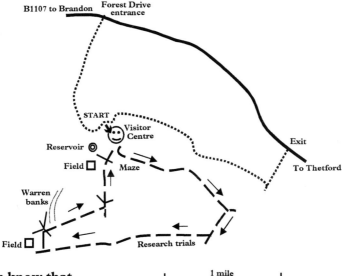

Did you know that...

High Lodge was a farm in the 19th century and if you look closely among the trees in the vicinity of Oak Lodge (an education and conference centre opened in 2003) you may glimpse fragments of the bricks from long-lost buildings scattered around. The census for 1861 records six dwellings here, housing the families of Matthews, Crowther, Little, Basham, Chapman and Wells, numbering nearly

3

thirty men, women and children. Their life would have been hard and this area very remote, even from the then tiny town of Brandon nearby. In the 1930s a labour camp was established here and unemployed men sent to work in the forest for their pay were housed in wooden huts. In turn the huts were used as Forest Offices in the 1950s and 60s and, when the BBC was filming 'Dad's Army' in the area, the remains of the hutted camp were used in some of the outdoor shots. It is sobering to think that this area has for so many years been a place of relentless hard toil where people eked out an existence and is now a place of leisure, giving enjoyment to thousands of people every year.

Scots and Corsican pines are the main species grown in Thetford Forest. Scots pine is a native of the British Isles and is recognised by the reddish colour of its bark and the blue green of its foliage. Corsican pine originates on the island of Corsica in the Mediterranean and it grows surprisingly well in the south and east of England considering the warmer climate it is used to in its native land. It can be distinguished from the Scots pine by the greyer bark and darker green of its needles. The foresters here prefer the Corsican pine because it grows faster, suffers less from diseases and because of the superior straightness of the stems of the trees. Around 2,400 trees are planted per hectare, which is about 1,000 trees to the acre. By the time the plantations are mature there will be around 500 large trees per hectare, the rest having been removed by thinning out during the 55-year crop rotation. At the end of the rotation the trees are felled for their valuable timber, which is used for construction and fencing purposes, and the site is replanted.

The process of felling and replanting creates a constantly changing mosaic of different aged crops throughout the forest and this habitat diversity is of special value to a host of plant, bird and animal species. **Woodlarks and nightjars** are very rare species on an international scale and this type of forest habitat suits them well, the forest being home to a significant proportion of the British breeding populations each summer. For this reason the forest is now designated a **Special Protection Area**, an international status, which means it must continue to be managed in particular for the benefit of these species.

Where the soils are shallower and more alkaline the crops may be damaged by **conifer butt rot fungus**, which is transmitted from tree to tree by root contact. On areas where the presence of this fungus is

4

significant, the stumps are dug out before the new crop is planted, and you will see places where this has happened. The lines of stumps raked up across the sites are known as windrows.

The long low banks mentioned in the walk are the remains of the boundary banks of ancient rabbit warrens. **High Lodge warren** was a particularly large warren where rabbits were farmed from medieval times up until the end of the 19th century. The banks marked the boundaries between warrens and, when in use, would have been much higher and steeper sided. Gorse was grown along the tops and this made it difficult for the rabbits to climb over. Of course they could burrow through the soft sand of the banks but it seemed that as long as food was plentiful they had no real incentive to try to escape. Some of the banks were flint-lined as well.

The **Research Trials** were planted in the 1950s and 60s to help advise on which other species might grow well here. Larch and Douglas fir can be grown but are slow to establish and prone to damage or killing by the late spring frosts that make the Brecks notorious. Over the years ground frosts have been recorded on every night of the year, as the sandy soil loses its heat so quickly at night. Perhaps global warming will mean that in the future different species will be more successful here.

It is still just possible, though sadly not very likely, that you may see a **red squirrel** on your walk. Once very numerous, the native red squirrel has largely been displaced from its home by the larger grey squirrel, which was introduced from North America to the London parks late in the 19th century and quickly spread out and across the country. There are very few red squirrels left in Thetford Forest now and their grey cousins are pushing them further and further north. Nowadays you will generally need to go to central Scotland and beyond if you are to stand a good chance of seeing one. Thetford Forest Park chose the red squirrel as its emblem when it was created in 1999, in recognition of the fact that the forest has been a refuge for large numbers of this beautiful native animal for so many years.

2. St Helen's Picnic Place

Grid reference for start TL827873   *Distance 2 miles*

This short walk, starting from Saint Helen's picnic place in the heart of the forest near Santon Downham, uses good paths and takes you along the banks of the River Little Ouse.

The easiest way to reach St Helen's Picnic Place is to take the A134 King's Lynn road from Thetford town and, after about four miles, turn left down a narrow lane through the forest signed Santon Downham. After a mile or so you will cross a railway line and within 100 yards turn left down an even narrower lane with passing places. This will lead you to the Picnic Place where there are car parking, toilet facilities, picnic tables and children's play equipment all on an attractive grassed area beside the River Little Ouse. You can also reach this spot from the B1107 Thetford to Brandon road where you should aim for Santon Downham village, which is well signed off this road. Once in the village, go downhill beside the church. Go carefully through the narrow bend between buildings and shortly you will cross the river. A hundred yards or so after the river, turn right down the narrow road with passing places.

The Walk

Start your walk by going back to the entrance to the car park and looking for the narrow wooden footbridge, which spans the Little Ouse. Cross the river and follow the fenced footpath where it passes between two small fields. At the T-junction of paths turn right and follow this wider track through the forest ignoring the turning on the left. After a short distance the track becomes a stony forest road and climbs gently uphill to reach a lane. This lane is the entrance road into Santon Downham village from the Thetford road. A magnificent avenue of ancient lime trees borders it at this point. Turn right and follow the lane to the church where you turn right again and go downhill past the Headquarters of the Forestry Commission team that manages this wonderful forest.

Walk carefully through the narrow lane where it bends between buildings and you will soon come to a white painted steel bridge over the Little Ouse. Cross the bridge and immediately take the steps on your right down to the path along the river. This was the towing path in an age when the river was navigable to Thetford and horse-drawn

6

barges brought goods up and down the river. Follow the grassy towpath back to the picnic place where you started your walk.

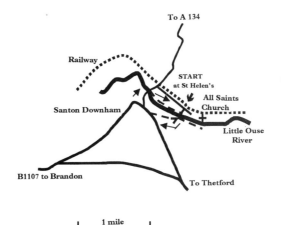

Did you know that...

St Helen's picnic place is one of a number of picnic places dotted throughout the forest. There are toilet facilities here, though not all the picnic places have this facility. Within the grassed area of St Helens is a fenced-off area of rough grass and small bushes. There are curious ditches and banks here which are the moated remains of **Santon House**, a large manor house, part of the long-deserted village of Santon which stood in this area.

A surfaced, all-weather path, designed for use by **disabled visitors** makes a circuit of the picnic area along the river bank and climbs gently to reach the higher ground of the picnic area near the railway line.

At the far end of the parking and picnic area at St Helens is the tiny **church of All Saints, Santon**, which has recently been restored and may be open at weekends in the summer. The original church on this site was built in 1628 and restored and enlarged to its present size in 1858 by the Revd William Weller-Poley. You can reach it either by walking along the lane, which passes through the picnic area, or by using the surfaced path along the riverbank.

The **River Little Ouse** was navigable to Thetford in the 19th century but fell into disuse when the railway was built in 1845. There were no locks on the river and to generate sufficient depth of water for the barges a series of staunches were built at intervals along the river between Thetford and Brandon. A staunch was like a simple dam lowered across the river allowing water to back up behind it, thus increasing its depth. Barges would be let through by simply lifting the dam and allowing them to be carried through on a wave of deeper water. A simple enough matter when going downstream but much more difficult going upstream when the horses that pulled the barges would have had to work hard against the relatively strong flow through the staunch. Once through, of course, the dam would be lowered to maintain the depth of water and the force of the water eased off. Nowadays the river is much shallower and more heavily silted up compared to when it was a navigation.

The stony road which you climbed after crossing the river footbridge is known as the **Military Road**. During the Second World War the area was heavily occupied by the military that were here to support the many British and American air bases in this part of East Anglia; this area was used for the storage of munitions.

The forest village of **Santon Downham** was originally known as Downham St Mary and changed its name to Santon Downham in the 17th century. Once an estate village built around Downham Hall, it was developed to its present size by the Forestry Commission to provide housing for some of the men and their families during the early development of Thetford Forest. Downham Hall was in poor condition when the Commission purchased the estate and was demolished between 1925 and 1927. Nearly all the older flint buildings, which survive in the village, were once part of that great estate.

The **church of St Mary** in Santon Downham village is 12th century and well worth a visit. It has a 13th century font and 14th century Screen. The tower was built between 1460 and 1500. Most of the stained glass is more modern, being largely Victorian in origin.

There are no pubs in the village but confectionery and drinks can be purchased from the village shop at the bottom of the hill from the church. There are more toilet facilities at the foot of the hill and also a car park for the Forestry Commission offices, which can also be used at weekends.

3. Walking the Little Ouse Path

Grid reference of start TL869830   *Distance 10 miles*

This is an interesting walk between the Breckland towns of Thetford and Brandon which, for much of the route, follows the banks of the Little Ouse River. Due to the length of the route only the most determined will walk the route in both directions on the same occasion. However, one solution to the problem is to check the train timetable and arrange your walk so that you can use the train to bring you back to your starting point. You can obtain a leaflet about the walk, which is clearly way-marked along its route, at local tourist information centres and the Forestry Commission headquarters in Santon Downham. There are information boards at the start of the walk in Thetford or Brandon and also at the Santon Downham offices. There are also public toilets in Santon Downham on the route of the walk.

The start of the walk in Thetford is at the main car park and bus station by the riverside in the town centre. If you start from Brandon you may find limited kerbside parking in the High Street or you could use the station car park or one of the town centre car parks. This description of the walk assumes you are starting the walk from Thetford.

The Walk

Walk from the car park towards the Town Bridge and, crossing the road, walk down to the towing path, (or haling path as it is known locally), alongside the river. At this point the path is tarmac and easy to follow. It goes beneath a main road emerging beside a riverside parkland area from which can be glimpsed the ruins of Thetford Priory on the other side of the river. Keep to the river's edge and after a short distance cross the river on Blaydon Bridge footbridge and continue the walk downstream along the riverbank. Leaving the tarmac path walk under another road bridge and, keeping to the same side of the river, continue along the towpath.

Before long, your journey takes you under one final bridge that carries the main A11 Thetford by-pass overhead. Soon you begin to leave the noise of traffic behind and feel you are getting into the peace of the countryside. The towpath is mainly a grassed path of varying width for some distance. A landmark is the sluice gates and weir across the river.

9

After a quarter of a mile or so this path moves slightly away from the river to avoid a marshy area of tall poplar and willow trees and turns to run parallel with the river along the edge of a pine plantation. Keep straight ahead, ignoring the occasional side turning, as the path curves gently following the bends of the river, which is barely visible through the scrubby woodland on your left.

A mile or so further on, conspicuous in front of you across open ground as you leave the pines, is the tall chimney of the Thetford Power station. Picking up the river bank again, the path runs along squeezed in between the river and the Power Station and emerges as a grass track near a small boat-launching ramp close to the Scout and Guide Headquarters building. It then narrows to single file as it approaches a steel footbridge over which you cross the river.

After you cross the bridge, follow the path as it winds through the tall poplars before climbing steeply up onto the drier ground of the forest with a wide, heather-covered ride in front of you. At the first crossing of tracks turn right and follow the path until, about 100 yards from a field, you turn left on to a narrow track through a pine plantation. Soon you reach a fenced field and turning left you follow the boundary of the forest for about 200 yards before turning right to head off across the field. Often there are horses to be seen here. The footpath goes straight across the field with a fence on the right and re-enters the forest via a sandy track that bears slightly right as it goes gently downhill into the trees.

Cross a sandy road and follow this path through the trees, turning left onto a wider path, which you follow for some distance with fields visible through the trees to your right. After about three quarters of a mile, and shortly after a footpath with fences on either side has joined on the right, the track becomes a stony forest road and climbs gently uphill to reach a lane. This lane is the entrance road into Santon Downham village from the Thetford road. It is bordered at this point by a magnificent avenue of ancient lime trees. Turn right and follow the lane to the Church where you turn right again and go downhill past the Headquarters of the Forestry Commission team that manages this wonderful forest.

Walk carefully through the narrow lane where it bends between buildings and you will soon come to a white-painted steel bridge over the Little Ouse. Cross the bridge and immediately take the steps on your left down to the path along the river.

Most of the remainder of the walk is now a path along the bank of the river. In places the path is narrow and slightly rough but in

10

general the walking is easy and takes you through one of the quietest areas of forest to be found. On your way you will pass reedy areas, and here you are likely to hear duck and geese calling and glimpse a heron or perhaps even a kingfisher.

As you approach Brandon you will begin to see houses and buildings across the river and, soon after crossing a small footbridge over a dyke, you begin to come into the outskirts of the town.

Passing a small mooring platform, which marks the official limit of the Little Ouse Navigation for boats, the path turns right, away from the river and is a narrow fenced path at the rear of houses and flats. It comes out into the housing area and you turn left down a residential road to emerge onto the High Street close to the town bridge. Turning left takes you to the town centre and turning right it is about a quarter of a mile to the railway station and the return journey to Thetford.

Enjoy the train journey back as you rest your weary legs. The train whisks you back through the forest and you will recognise many of the areas where you walked a few hours ago.

There are plenty of places to choose from to eat in Brandon and Thetford and both towns are quite small and can be explored on foot easily. You may also get refreshments from the village store in Santon Downham, the shop being open at usual hours. The shop is beside the Forestry Commission Headquarters.

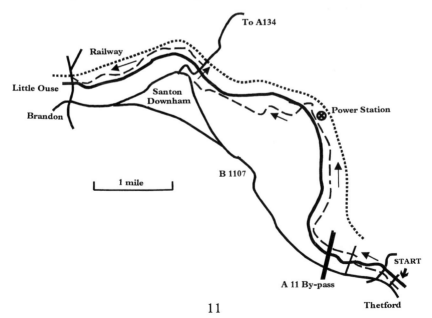

11

Did you know that....

Thetford town is full of history and is a very ancient borough. At one time it was the largest and most important town in East Anglia, surpassing even Norwich. There are many old buildings, churches

and ruins to explore. The cast iron Town Bridge, constructed in 1829, is tastefully painted to create a colourful crossing of the river. Modern day Thetford is founded on industry and started to grow to its present size when it became a London over-spill town in the 1960s. Once home to the most famous steam traction engine manufacturer in the world, the Burrell Steam museum is open to the public and well worth a visit.

The Forestry Commission has declared the whole length of the land in its ownership along the Little Ouse valley a **Forest Nature Reserve**. This means it is recognised and managed for the benefit of the wide range of habitats and wildlife that it contains.

The **Thetford power station** is the largest of its type in Britain. It produces 38.5 megawatts of electricity, (enough for a town of 93,000 houses or five times the size of Thetford), by burning poultry litter from the many poultry farms in East Anglia and wood chips produced from forest waste in Thetford Forest. Each year around 450,000 tonnes of such material is burnt.

The modern **Santon Downham village** was largely built by the Forestry Commission in the early days of Thetford Forest to provide housing for forestry workers and their families in the heart of the forest. Nowadays most of the residents work elsewhere but the village is prettily placed around its large green and worth a short detour. Amongst the modern dwellings are a number of older flint properties which were part of the original Downham Hall estate.

Brandon was once home to two unique industries, both of which have long since ended. First, it had two **rabbit factories** where rabbits from the Breckland warrens were brought to be processed for their fur. This fur was used extensively in the manufacture of felt to make bowler and top hats in particular. The meat was also used and sent far afield for sale. In fact, as many as 30,000 rabbit carcases a year were sent to London alone in the 1850s. The second industry was **flint-knapping**; locally dug flint was 'knapped' or worked not only to make flints for building construction but also to make flints for flintlock muskets, which were exported all over the world. The latter trade, which was practised, among other places in the yard at the rear of the Flintknappers public house, died out finally in the 1950s. The Brandon Heritage Centre in the town will explain more about both of these industries.

Saint Mary's church in Santon Downham is well worth a visit. A church is recorded on the site in the Domesday Book, though this was a wooden predecessor. The present church was started in the 12th century with the tower being constructed between 1460 and 1500. Inside there is a 13th or 14th century font. Most of the stained glass is of Victorian date. The altar cross, candlesticks and processional cross are all made of wood, worked by a local forester.

13

4. Roudham Heath and the Peddars Way

Grid reference for start TL 957858   *Distance 8 miles*

The start of this walk is in The Street in the village of Bridgham. To reach the village, leave Thetford by the Norwich Road. Look out for the large supermarket on your right and take the right turn signposted Kilverstone and Brettenham. Follow this quite narrow lane for about five miles and you will arrive in the village. Park carefully in The Street near to the parish church of Saint Mary the Virgin.

The Walk

Walk along The Street with the church on your right and after a hundred yards or so turn left into Timber Hill. Soon the road forks with Timber Hill going off to the left, signposted High Bridgham. Take the right fork, Back Lane, signposted Roudham, and follow the lane as it twists and curves gently uphill for about a mile.

After a while, the lane bears sharp right with the ruined church of St Andrew, once the parish church for the lost mediaeval village of Roudham, a short distance along on the left. At this point the lane meets with three other tracks or drives to form a crossroads. You will need to take the driveway that appears straight in front of you, signposted as a public path. However, before you do so, you can walk the short distance to explore the ruins of the church and its little graveyard.

After visiting the church, walk down the concrete driveway between houses and soon the drive becomes a track between fields and crosses the railway line. In the distance you will see and hear the traffic on the busy A11 Norwich road. The track joins a modern road that passes under the A11 by means of a subway and climbs steeply up the other side to emerge on the boundary between fields and Roudham Forest.

At the highest point of the tarmac road, continue ahead on the sandy track along the edge of the forest until you reach a steel communications tower. Beside the tower turn left and go through a gap in the bank to enter Roudham Forest. Initially you are on a chalky track but this soon joins a stony forest road. The road goes ahead through the forest along the edge of a field on your left. Near the end of the field, fork right along a wide grassy ride and where this ride meets more fields, turn left along the forest edge until you reach

14

another track by a gas pumping station. Turn left and follow this road downhill to the railway and its level crossing. You are now walking the Peddars Way, a long-distance footpath running from Knettishall Heath about 5 miles in front of you, to the Norfolk Coast at Hunstanton about forty miles behind you.

Very carefully cross the railway line taking care to close both wicket gates behind you and walk straight ahead to reach the A11 again. This time you have to cross over the dual carriageway with the greatest care as this is a fast and busy major road. Once across, the Peddars Way continues straight ahead with pine plantations on your left and Brettenham Heath on your right. After about half a mile the track crosses a quiet lane near High Bridgham.

Here you have a choice. If you turn left and walk down the lane you will return to Timber Hill in Bridgham Village about a mile away. Alternatively press on straight ahead along the Peddars Way still with forest and heath to left and right.

The Peddars Way is easy to follow and is well signposted through a mixture of plantations, small woodlands and fields before it descends gently into the valley where it meets a quiet country lane.

Cross this lane and continue on the Peddars Way along a narrow hedged section, which then joins a wooden boardwalk across a marshy area to reach a bridge over the River Thet. Cross the bridge, go down the steps and turn hard left along the bank of the river. Follow the somewhat rough path close to the water's edge. Soon the path rises onto slightly higher and drier ground and you will see a small field beyond a ditch on your right. This field is used as an overflow area to the Forestry Commission's Thorpe Woodlands campsite during the summer season. Turn right and away from the river at the end of the field and follow the field edge for a short distance, going round a pole barrier on the left and onto a gravel track past a farmhouse, also on the left. Bear left past the front of the farmhouse and take the second exit left onto a stony road with the main campsite on the right. This track leads to houses, but near the far corner of the camp site take the path off to the right which goes through trees before joining a grassy path with a fence on the left.

Keep to this track, which follows a signed footpath twisting and curving and keeping to firm ground along the edge of marshy ground close to the River Thet with a fence on your left along its entire distance. After about a mile the track re-enters woodland on both sides before following the edge of a small field on your left to lead out onto a sandy track.

Turn left and follow this track as it drops down to cross the River Thet. Immediately after crossing the second bridge over the River Thet, turn right over a footbridge and a stile into a small field. Cross this field diagonally, heading towards a large white-gabled house on the hill in front of you, and so back to the start of your walk.

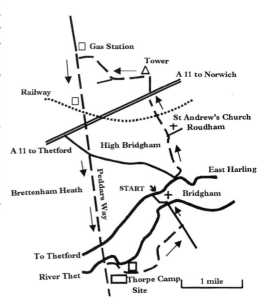

Did you know that...

Bridgham is probably a very old settlement and its name means 'a settlement by a bridge'.

The church of **Saint Mary the Virgin in Bridgham** is mainly 14th century though records show a church has been here since Saxon times. The wooden bell-turret at the west end of the nave houses a single bell from 1632. A visiting historian recorded 'the steeple down' in 1735 but there are no records to confirm when it fell. Inside, the 15th century font is particularly ornate with carved figures around the eight major compass points. It has a 17th century cover.

The ruined **church of Saint Andrew** was built in the 14th century and fell into disuse around 1735 after a disastrous fire. A workman repairing the tower set the thatched roof alight when ashes fell from his pipe. A few years ago the ruins were almost totally covered in ivy, giving the church the appearance of a weird sculpture, but this has now been removed and the fine brick and flint work can be enjoyed again.

The deserted medieval village of **Roudham** was in the fields down the slope behind the church. A smart new shelter, built to commemorate the millennium, stands in Roudham village close to the ruined church. It provides good protection from the weather and makes a fine picnic spot with seating to face any aspect. Interpretation panels on the walls of the shelter give more detailed information about the shrunken medieval village and the ruined church.

The tall steel mast on the edge of the woods at Roudham Forest after you emerge from the underpass was once a **Forestry Commission fire look-out tower**. From its position at the top of the hill the tower would have afforded an excellent view over much of the eastern part of Thetford Forest. It is now a radio and telecommunications tower.

The **Peddars Way** is nearly 50 miles in length. It is an ancient track-way, probably in existence before the Romans, although they modified and improved it in true Roman fashion In places the construction of the road with its cambered surface and shallow drainage gullies either side, (known as the *agger*), can still be seen. A particularly well-preserved, embanked section of the *agger* is visible for a short distance south of Brettenham Heath. It is now one of the long-distance national trails, which criss-cross much of England, and connects with the North Norfolk Coast Path, which begins near Hunstanton. The Way varies from narrow footpath to wide grassy track as you travel its length. You can walk another section of the Peddars Way in Walk 13 in this booklet.

Thorpe Woodlands campsite is operated by the Forestry Commission. It is a simple site but most of the pitches have electric hook-up points and it is popular with caravanners seeking a clean, basic site in a quiet and restful location.

5. High Lodge and Santon Downham

Grid reference for start TL816876   *Distance 6 miles*

This walk links the main High Lodge Visitor Centre to the village of Santon Downham. High Lodge offers a range of visitor attractions and there are refreshment and toilet facilities available. Walk 1 in this booklet contains further information about everything it has to offer. Around Santon Downham village the walk passes through magnificent Douglas firs which are regenerating freely and make an interesting contrast with the pine forest predominating over the rest of the area. The start of the walk is at High Lodge, which is very well signed off the Thetford to Brandon road (B1107), and also signed from further afield by the familiar brown tourist signs. There are public toilets at the Forestry Commission car park in Santon Downham, which is about half way round this walk. The adjacent village shop offers friendly service for snacks and soft drinks.

The Walk

Walk away from the main Visitor Centre building and head diagonally right across the large grass picnic and play area to where a stony track leaves this arena passing the end of a row of huge lime trees with another smaller building off to your left. Follow this track until it reaches a stony forest road with a large, circular, concrete reservoir on your right. Turn right along this road, passing the almost hidden circular pond known as the Horseshoe Pit on your left.

The stony road meets the tarmac Forest Drive heading to the Visitor Centre and you need to walk straight ahead looking out for oncoming traffic.

After a while, the Drive bears right on a sweeping bend and here you take a grassy track on the left behind a pole barrier leading you away into the trees. Keep straight ahead, ignoring all side turnings, until you come to a fork in the path. Take the left hand fork, which is a less well-used path, and where it reaches the boundary between the forest and other woodland, turn right along the remnants of an old fence line. You will see a field through the trees to your left. Please be aware that the land on the left is in private ownership and is not open to the public. After half a mile or so the footpath runs along the edge of the forest with a wooden boarded fence on the right and leads you out by a public road next to a housing estate on the outskirts of Brandon.

This road meets with the busier Brandon to Thetford road, which you need to cross, aiming for another minor lane which heads away to the right leading back towards Santon Downham. Leaving the last of the houses on the left on this lane, look for the signed footpath going steeply down into the trees on the left.

Follow this footpath, which crosses the entrance road to two cottages in the forest and later crosses another sandy track. Go straight over this track and keep ahead for about half a mile on a wider grassy and heather-covered ride. Your path then crosses a stony forest road and you need to take the next turning right after this, and after a short distance bear left, along a tree-lined path through mixed woodland.

This path leads you to the village of Santon Downham, emerging onto the large village green beside the village hall. Continue ahead with houses on your left until you reach the public road that skirts the green. Follow this road until you reach the church and then turn left downhill, signed Santon Warren, to reach the car park beside the Forestry Commission offices and village shop.

With the car park on your left continue walking downhill between cottages on a bend in the lane. On crossing the white-painted steel bridge over the River Little Ouse, immediately go down the steps on the right to walk upstream along the riverside path.

After a while you will reach a narrow wooden footbridge over the river. Cross here and follow the path between fences until you reach a wider, stony forest road. Here, turn right and almost immediately left to climb the hill on a grassy ride. At the top of the hill the path meets a lane bordered by an avenue of lime trees.

Cross straight over and the path narrows through mixed woodland and shortly meets with a stony forest road. Turn left onto the stony road and after about thirty yards or so take the path right through the Douglas Firs. Keep to this path ignoring all side turnings until you reach another stony forest road.

Turn left along this road, which is bordered with belts of oak and beech trees on either side until you reach a main road.

Cross straight over to the start of the Forest Drive which leads to High Lodge and follow the Drive a short distance to the point where power cables cross it. Here turn left onto a grassy track and then take the first turning on the right.

The path climbs gently uphill for some distance and you follow this, ignoring turnings to right and left. Where the slope levels out you meet another path crossing in front of you. Turn right and almost immediately left and follow this round, turning left again beside broadleaved woodland to arrive in one of the car parks at High Lodge where you will see the Visitor Centre through the trees ahead.

You will have earned a rest after the walk and this is a delightful place to stop and have a breather with so much to see and do.

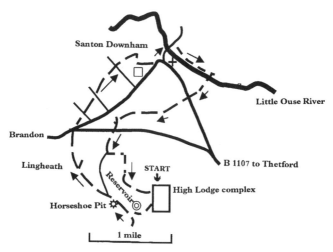

Did you know that...

Great Britain has only three native species of conifer and of these only the **Scots Pine** is widely planted for its timber value. In consequence all the other conifer species grown commercially in UK forests are imports from North America, Europe or Japan and we are fortunate that the British climate is so well suited to the growth of trees from such a wide area of the world. **Douglas Fir** was introduced from the Pacific coast of north-west America in 1827 by David Douglas who was an explorer and plant hunter responsible for the introduction of over 240 species of plants to this country. In its native habitat it grows up to 300 feet in height. Although this species originates from a

20

maritime region where rainfall is very much higher than that of East Anglia, the Douglas Firs around Santon Downham have grown surprisingly well and these, at around 80 years of age and 100 feet in height, should grow on for a good while yet.

High Lodge is aptly named as it is situated on the top of one of the highest points around. The concrete reservoir contains water, which is supplied to Brandon and the neighbouring area.

Horseshoe Pit was an Iron Age village site between 880 BC and 42 AD followed by Early Roman occupancy to 409 AD. The almost continuous supply of water here is the most likely reason why this site developed. Items such as pottery sherds, a Roman knife and bronze stylus, found during excavations, have helped date the site, and the finds are now in Ipswich museum. Nowadays the site tends to dry up in summer weather, probably due to silting of the pit since it fell into disuse. However it is a valuable asset to local wildife, providing a breeding location for toads and other amphibians. Further evidence of continued human habitation of the area is derived from a 1791 estate map showing field names such as Brick Kiln Brakes and Thetford Brakes while the area around the present High Lodge is shown as Sheepswalk. The site of Brick Kiln cottage is a little way down the Forest Drive on the right as you walk towards Brandon, the site being marked by scrubby trees and mounds of earth and spoil containing fragments of old brickwork.

The stretch of the walk after you leave the forest drive, heading along the forest edge towards the housing estates at Brandon, borders **Lingheath Farm**. Here there were very large numbers of flint pits, (estimated at around 2,000 pits originally), sunk into the ground where miners extracted flint to be 'knapped' or worked for building construction and decoration, or fashioned into flints for flintlock muskets. This work was carried on until as recently as the 1930s and, unlike the complex of pits at nearby Grimes Graves (see Walk 17 in this booklet), they were narrow shafts, each worked by no more than one or two individual miners. The last miner working for a living on Lingheath was 'Pony' Ashley of Brandon. Brandon was the major centre for **flint-knapping** for over two hundred years with flint products exported world wide. Nowadays the main visual evidence for the pits is little more than sunken depressions in the soil and the occasional heap of partially-worked and discarded flints, though these are mainly lost in the vegetation.

6. The King's Forest and the Icknield Way

Grid reference for start TL815715　　　*Distance 13 miles*

This is one of the longest walks in this book with good paths throughout and, although the walking is mainly in the forest, there is a sense of open country about much of the route.

The most convenient starting place is at the Forestry Commission car park at West Stow. The car park is reached from the B1106 Brandon to Bury St Edmunds road. About five miles south of the A11 at Elveden the B1106 road turns very sharply to the left. At this point turn right very carefully onto the minor road signposted West Stow and Country Park. Follow this lane around for about half a mile and take the first turning right, passing through the tiny village of West Stow. Where the houses finish on the right, turn right along a tarmac drive with a farm on the right and forest on the left. The small car park is at the end of this drive opposite a house. You can also reach the car park from the A1101 Mildenhall to Bury St Edmunds road. From Mildenhall, soon after you pass through Icklingham village, look for the turning to your left signed West Stow and follow this for about two miles. As you come into West Stow village the tarmac road is on your left.

The Walk

From the car park walk ahead into the forest passing an office and shed on your right. Take the first stony forest road on the left. Keep to this stony road straight ahead for about a mile and you will reach the Icknield Way. Turn right and follow the Way as it climbs gently into The King's Forest. For most of its length it is a sandy track wandering between wide, grassy and heathy verges with mixed woodland beyond. You now simply forge ahead for about three undulating miles ignoring all tracks and forest roads to left and right.

Towards the end of the three miles and just before the Way comes alongside a field surrounded by the forest on all sides, look for a wide grassy ride which forks right here, through a pole barrier, and diverges gently away from the Icknield Way itself. I recommend this slight diversion as this ride is pleasant to walk on and is a lovely avenue with beech plantations on either side. At the end of the avenue go round the pole barrier and you will find yourself on a small triangular grassy area next to the main road. There is a small flint monument here commemorating the planting of Queen Mary's Avenue, which you have just walked along. To your left the Icknield way rejoins, having skirted the edge of the Beech trees adjacent to Queen Mary's Avenue.

Continue straight ahead past the monument and across the grassy area. Look for a narrow path running parallel to the main road, which is set back a few yards from the road itself behind a scrubby hedge-row. This allows you to walk the next short section of the route away from the danger of fast-moving traffic. This path brings you to a wide track with a byway sign. Cross the road to take another tarmac drive signed Icknield Way and Barrow Clump, which soon leaves the traffic noise behind as you head out between fields and trees.

Soon after you pass a farm on the left, the Icknield Way forks left at the corner of a field. However you need to take the turning on the right which you follow diagonally across fields to reach the edge of the King's Forest on your right. The path follows the boundary of the forest for some distance. Keep to the forest boundary, ignoring the signed track, which takes the Icknield Way off to your left, until you reach a house on your left. Here, look for the signed byway on the right just before a short section of low wall and follow this track down into the forest. Take the dog-leg left and the byway brings you out onto another stony track at the corner of a hedged field. At this corner, turn right on a grassy track through trees which then widens out into a wide grassy ride leading away into the forest again.

Take this track, which is known as Chalk Lane, and follow it straight ahead through the forest until you reach a main road. Do not go out onto the road. Instead, turn left off Chalk Lane and make your way down through the huge Corsican pine trees of the King's Forest picnic site. At the furthest end of the picnic site the access track reaches the main road. Cross straight over here and set off into the forest along another stony forest road. After a short distance, at a crossing of forest roads, turn left down another stony road and walk steadily downhill, ignoring all side turnings and passing a cottage on your right. Continue ahead and go straight over at the next crossing point with another stony road. Keep ahead, still descending gently, passing another stony road on your right.

Keep straight ahead at this point following the first length of your original route in reverse to arrive back at the car park.

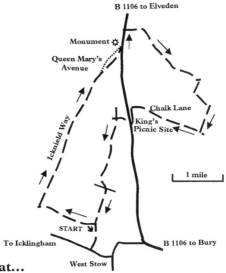

Did you know that...

The **Icknield Way** is an ancient trackway running from Ivinghoe Beacon in Buckinghamshire to Knettishall Heath in Norfolk, a distance of about 100 miles. It is thought to be the oldest road in England and certainly much of its length is pre-Roman. Archaeological features abound along its route as it follows the 'chalk spine' of England. In the south, it links to the Ridgeway National Trail and Wessex, while in Norfolk it joins the Peddars Way, another National Trail that crosses Norfolk to the coast near Hunstanton.

The King's Forest was created by the Forestry Commission in the mid 1930s, soon after it acquired the land from the Culford estate. The acquisition and early plantings coincided with the Silver Jubilee of King George V and Queen Mary in 1935 and the forest was given its name in honour of that occasion. At the north end of the forest, next to the Elveden to Bury St Edmunds road, the small flint-built monument with a plaque commemorates the occasion and the nearby wide, grass ride with beech plantations either side is named **Queen Mary's Avenue**. At one time, deeper into the forest, the letters G R were formed in the plantations by mixing beech trees into the pine plantations. It seems likely that the only people who ever saw this feature in this flat landscape would have been American airmen flying into the nearby Mildenhall air base.

Chalk Lane is rich in chalk-loving plants that grow profusely along its verges. Such a variety of plants also supports a diverse population of butterflies and other insects, some of which are scarce species.

The huge **Corsican pine** trees at the King's Forest picnic site are well over a hundred years old and were originally planted by the owners of the Culford Estate in the 1890s.

7. Lynford Stag and Lakes

Grid reference of start TL813918   *Distance 4 miles*

The start of this walk is at the car park for the Lynford Stag picnic area. This is next to the A134 Thetford to King's Lynn road, about a mile south east of Mundford village. The picnic area has toilets and play equipment for children. The car park takes its name from a steel stag, originally used as a shooting target by the Lynford estate, which was found by forestry workers many years ago. This stag was erected at the car park as a feature. More recently it has been joined by a giant deer made of timber, which is a play sculpture for children to climb in.

The Walk

Leave the car park by the wide avenue that runs back through the picnic area passing the small toilet block on the left. This track bears slightly right and then runs ahead as a long straight ride, initially through magnificent Douglas fir trees before coming out into younger plantations fringed by a young cedar avenue. The grassy ride eventually reaches a quiet country lane, which you cross to continue straight ahead along a straight, gravelled forest road.

At the end of this road there is another car park known as Zig-Zag Covert. Turn right here, still on the forest road with a fenced field on your left. At the corner of the field turn left and walk down a grassy path with the field still on your left. This will bring you to the first of the Lynford Lakes. If you were to go straight ahead you would cross a bridge over a stream and enter Lynford Arboretum. This is the subject of another walk in this booklet.

For this particular walk, turn left onto the surfaced path which skirts the edge of the lake on your right, with glimpses of Lynford Hall to be seen from time to time.

Keep along this path crossing another track and a bridge on your right. You will now be following a second lake known as the Long Water because it is long and narrow. At the end the Long Water opens out into a small lake.

At this point the surfaced path turns hard left back on itself but if you continue on ahead to the end of the lake you then turn left away from the lake on a grassy track under trees. This goes through a steel pole barrier and bears first right and then left, passing a secluded cottage on your right. You then join a track, which is the service road for the cottage, and begin to climb gently uphill through woodland on either side. At the top of the hill you again find the quiet country lane, which you cross to reach a forest road slightly to your right.

Walk up this straight, rather sandy road until at its end you turn left and almost immediately right on a wide grass path. Follow this path, again with tall Douglas firs on your left and younger pine trees on your right. Ignore any side turnings and after a while the path begins gently to bear left and you will see and hear traffic on the main road to your right. This path leads you back to the car park and picnic area at the start of your walk.

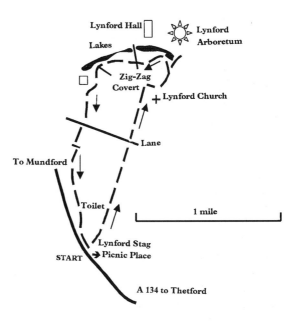

Did you know that...

The present **Lynford Hall** was built in 1857-62 replacing an earlier hall built in the early 18th century, which was destroyed by fire. It is a Grade II listed building in the Jacobean style and passed into the hands of the Forestry Commission when they purchased the estate in the 1924. It was used as a Forester Training School though this was closed in the 1950s. The original formal garden was constructed in the mid 19th century.

The adjoining **Lynford Arboretum** is a splendid collection of trees and there are surfaced paths throughout making it easy to visit for all ages. In the spring it is a mass of daffodils, snowdrops and bluebells. Many of the trees were planted by students from the Forester Training School in their spare time.

27

Lynford Hall and the surrounding area were used for much of the outdoor filming of **Dad's Army** and, more recently, **'Ello 'Ello**. The Long Water was used for filming some of the seaside shots of one particular Dad's Army episode.

Zig Zag Covert was where the pleasure gardens of the original Lynford Hall were situated. Although this particular walk does not go into the Covert it is possible to walk through it on another occasion. Within are remnants of the old gardens and some of the features such as statue bases, fountain pools and a short length of flint-walled tunnel.

8. Brandon Park and Shaker's Road

Grid reference for start TL 787852   *Distance 5 miles*

The start of this walk is at the Visitor Centre at Brandon Country Park, which is signed off the B1106 Elveden road on the outskirts of Brandon. There is free parking at the Country Park, which is open daily between dawn and dusk. The Country Park is owned by Suffolk County Council and jointly funded by Forest Heath District Council and there are a number of marked trails around the grounds of Brandon House and out into the surrounding Thetford Forest. These include easy access trails. This particular walk is my own route and you will need to follow my directions and ignore many of the way-marked paths in the area.

The Walk

The walk follows grassy tracks and forest roads throughout its length and is entirely within woodland. There are toilets and light refreshments available at the Visitor Centre, as well as picnic areas, a children's play area, a lake and walled gardens.

Visitor Centre opening times are 10.00 to 4.00 in the winter and 10.00 to 5.00 in the summer. Telephone 01842 810185 for more information.

From the main car park follow the signs to the Old Orchard picnic area and car park, passing the rear of Brandon Park house. From the small exit at the far corner of the Old Orchard take the short path through the trees to reach a grassy path with a Forest Enterprise sign in front of you. Turn left, uphill, with a house to your left, until you reach a turning to the right by an electricity pole. Keep to this grassy track, following the route of the electricity line and crossing over a stony forest road after about a mile. Continue straight ahead keeping to the grassy path to the bottom of the slope. Here, take the first grass track right followed by the first turning left. This track will bring you to another stony forest road and here you turn right. Go straight ahead, passing a large radio mast on the left hand side of the road and the signposted entrance to a bird hide also on the left. You can visit the bird hide if you wish, as it is only a short distance away.

From the radio mast continue along the main forest road with a short length of hedge on your right and take the first turning right at the end of the hedge, onto a sandy track. Follow this track, which at first is fairly level, and ignore all side turnings. At a T-junction near the brow of a hill the main track bears left and then continues along on the level for about two hundred yards. At this point the track divides into three and you need to take the central route, which drops away downhill, initially as a slightly sunken path. After about a quarter of a mile this track divides again and you then take the left fork. Follow this straight ahead and, ignoring all turnings left and right, follow this mainly sandy track for over a mile to the bottom of the hill where it meets a stony forest road at a junction. Turn right and go straight ahead, still on a stony stretch for a short distance, and then continuing ahead on a wide grassy or sandy stretch of track.

Ignore all side turnings and keep straight ahead for about half a mile. On the way your path will enter a fenced area and you pass close by a curious large mound on your left known as White Hill. Continue ahead until you reach another stony road crossing your route at a slight angle by an electricity line. Turn right and follow this track, which was once a carriage drive to Brandon House, until it brings you back uphill towards Brandon Country Park. You will see the mausoleum to your left and a signed path takes you past this, back into the grounds of the Country Park where you started your walk.

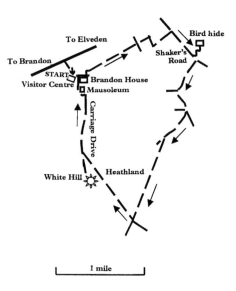

Did you know that...

Brandon House was built in 1826 by Edward Bliss. It originally had 21 bedrooms and stabling for 17 horses. The Forestry Commission bought the house in 1927 when it acquired parts of the neighbouring land for forestry and the USAAF used the house for transit accommodation for eleven years from 1956. It is now a nursing home

30

run by BUPA. Edward Bliss set out to plant an exotic tree garden from 1821 and this is why this part of the forest has so many old and unusual specimen trees today.

The tall radio mast you will pass on your walk is an important communications aerial for the police and other civil services as well as for telegraphy purposes. This part of the forest is known as **Mayday** and the road past the mast is a public footpath called **Shaker's Road** which would eventually lead you out onto heathland at Lakenheath Warren were you to follow it. Shaker's Road probably takes its name from 'Shakland', an East Anglian term for pasture where sheep graze.

White Hill is a bell barrow, an ancient earthwork dating to the Early and Middle Bronze Age around 1500 to 1100 BC. It is a scheduled ancient monument and is unusual because of its extraordinary size. Unusually, it is partly encircled by a ditch and bank, which is fairly easy to see. It would have been constructed as a mound covering a single or multiple burial. It is also unusual because bell barrows are nationally rare, the greatest concentration of them occurring in Wessex. The foresters have cleared the trees off the mound and it is now a component of the open heathland in the depth of the forest.

Your route takes you past a large fenced area of **heathland** where you may find cattle or sheep grazing at various times of the year. This area is being managed for its heathland flora by grazing and here heather is the dominant plant because of the deep, acid, sandy soils in the area. The heather is a spectacular sight in the late summer when it is in full flower.

The Carriage Drive takes you past the old **Mausoleum** where Edward Bliss and his wife were originally interred. Their remains were moved to St Peter's church-yard in Brandon early in the 1900s. It is a somewhat eerie old building enclosed in the brooding silence of the forest at this point. You may find this one of the noisier routes in this book as, for much of the time, you will be walking in an area of the forest close to **Lakenheath air base** and under the flight path into the airfield. By way of compensation you may get some spectacular views of some of the aircraft as they approach the base.

31

9. History at High Ash

Grid reference for start TL 813967   *Distance 3 miles*

The start of this walk must be the easiest of all to locate. Take the A1065 road from Mundford towards Swaffham and after about two miles you will see a Cromwell army tank sitting on top of a large brick plinth on your left. Park in the car park provided behind the tank.

The Walk

This short walk is on good paths and will take you around a part of the forest where modern and ancient history were made. The first part of the walk follows the signed route of a path set out by members of the Desert Rat Trust, the group responsible for the tank memorial at the entrance. The Caravan Club operates a camping site here and those who take caravan holidays may find this an attractive, central base to explore Thetford Forest Park and Breckland.

From the entrance to the car park walk ahead up the wide concrete road for a short distance. Once opposite the entrance to the Caravan Club site, turn left down a narrow track between dense pine trees. After only a hundred yards or so look for a narrow signed path going through the trees on your right. This turns left and right again to follow a track that brings you out onto a concrete path with older trees ahead of you. Turn right up this concrete path and keep your eye open for a number of small clearings with concrete areas amongst the trees on the left.

This was the site of a Second World War army camp where the Desert Rats carried out their training early in 1944 before taking part in the invasion of Europe in June 1944. The concrete areas were the bases for the army huts that formed the camp here.

At the top of the path you will rejoin the main concrete road, which again is a remnant of the wartime occupancy of the area. Turn left onto the concrete road and follow it as it bears right and descends a slight slope.

Keep straight ahead, climbing the gentle slope in front of you. A house is on the left and waterworks on the right. Opposite the house take the narrow concrete road to the right past the waterworks, and follow this, ignoring all side turnings, until you reach a main road. Turn left and, keeping safely to the wide grass verge, walk about 30 yards until you are opposite a track, which leads to a large tele-communications mast.

Cross the main road with care and walk down the track with the aerial on your left and keep straight ahead until you reach a crossing point of grass tracks. Your route turns right here, but before doing so take the left turning for about 20 yards and on your left, in a clearing in the pine trees, is the ruin of an old building with a plaque proclaiming it to be Langford Lodge.

Retrace your steps and follow the route described, the grass track dropping gently downhill where it meets a stony forest road. Keep straight ahead, turning right when you reach a T-junction and follow the forest road back to the main road. Here you are back at the start of the walk opposite the Cromwell tank. Cross this very fast stretch of road with care to reach the car park.

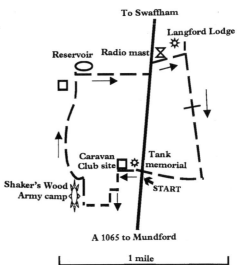

Did you know that....

The **7th Armoured Division** was formed in 1939 and played a major part in the defeat of Rommel's Africa Korps. After the success of the North African Campaign the Division returned to England and was based in Thetford Forest from January to May 1944 in preparation for its part in the Invasion of Europe. The Division sailed from Felixstowe on 5th June 1944 and landed on Gold Beach in Normandy in the evening of 6th June 1944, where it was heavily involved in the early fighting followed by the pursuit of the German Army across Europe and back to Berlin.

The Cromwell Tank had a crew of five men and was powered by a 600 hp Rolls Royce Meteor engine. Its design speed was 32 mph but it achieved a speed of over 50 mph during combat. It weighed over 27 tonnes and its main armament was a 75 mm gun supported by a pair of 7.92 mm machine guns. The memorial was constructed in 1998 and inaugurated at a ceremony on 23 October in that year.

The Desert Rat sign came into being in 1940 and was inspired by the jerboa, a species of rat found in the North African desert where the Division had such memorable successes in the North Africa Campaign. This sign is also used to mark the way-marked paths set out in the forest for visitors by the Desert Rats Trust

Langford Lodge is very much a ruin with only the stump of one corner left standing to give any sense of what the building looked like. It is a late medieval building, possibly 15th century, and was probably a warreners' lodge similar to the one still standing near the golf course at Thetford. Now surrounded by pine trees, it is difficult to imagine how lonely a spot this must have been 300 years or so ago when it was isolated by the surrounding heath, while its residents eked out a living farming rabbits in the local warrens. Langford Lodge was marked on Faden's map of Norfolk of 1797 and so we must assume it to have been still inhabited at that date.

10. Lynford Stag and West Tofts

Grid reference for start TL813918   *Distance 6 miles*

This walk starts from the car park and picnic place at Lynford Stag, one mile south of Mundford village on the A134 road towards Thetford. The car park is well signed and there are public toilets available here as well.

The Walk

From the rear of the main car park section which is under the trees, walk out onto the grass track along which the power line runs. Turn right and after about a hundred yards turn left along a grassy track through tall pine trees. Ignore any side turnings until you reach a sandy forest road on the right. Turn right and follow this road until you come to a lane. On the way you will pass an area on the right with an unusual variety of trees, which is a research area.

Go straight across the lane onto another stony forest road that becomes a grassy track after some distance. Follow this until you reach another stony road that crosses in front of you. Turn left and follow this hard road for about half a mile until you reach a point where another stony road goes off to the right. At this point take the grass ride to the left and follow this out across fields, passing a farm on the left and going straight ahead until you reach a tarmac road. This is a public road but is usually fairly quiet as it is not a through-road for traffic, other than military traffic going to and from the adjacent army training area. Turn left along this lane with houses and the army training area boundary on your right for about another half a mile.

You will then come to West Tofts army camp on your left, followed soon after by a crossroads. Keep straight ahead and follow this lane, which may be a little busier along this section. After half a mile or so you will pass houses on either side followed soon after by a small field on the right. At the far end of the field, forest roads go off to right and left. Take the left turn onto a stony forest road with an avenue of young cedar trees on either side and keep straight on for about 150 yards. Look for a small turning on the right that is rather narrow and can be overlooked. Follow this path for a short distance and then turn left. Keep straight ahead ignoring all paths right and left until you come to a rather shaded track with large beech trees in front of you. Turn right and then left after a short distance and follow the grass path back to the car park with the main road through the trees to your right.

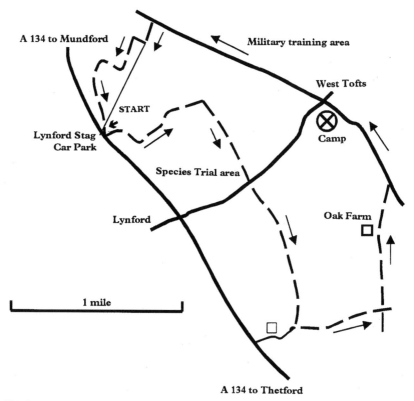

A 134 to Mundford

Military training area

West Tofts

START

Lynford Stag Car Park

Camp

Species Trial area

Lynford

Oak Farm

1 mile

A 134 to Thetford

Did you know that...

The large military training area often referred to locally as the **Battle Area,** is used by the army to train troops for a wide range of modern warfare. The military authorities commandeered much of the area during the Second World War and a number of villages were evacuated completely. The area has remained in the jurisdiction of the army since then. Occasionally, organised tours take place and give members of the public a chance to glimpse a little of the history of the area. Enquire at local libraries or Tourist Information Centres about such tours. As well as being a major training area, the Battle Area is renowned for its conservation value, being one of the largest areas of Breckland heath remaining intact today.

The BBC filmed many of the outdoor scenes from **Dad's Army** on the Battle Area. The closing sequence was filmed on Frog Hill, which is a short distance into the Battle Area along the road described in this walk. Jones' old butcher's van was frequently filmed on the roads that are now within the training area. Another well-known television series filmed in this part of the world was 'Ello, 'Ello, the fictional story of French resistance during the Second World War.

The **Research plots** mentioned in the walk are worth a look as you pass by. The area is one of a series of such trial areas planted when the forest was first being planted in the 1920s and 30s to test a range of different species for their success in the Breckland conditions.

Although no longer actively managed by the Forestry Commission's Research Division, this is an interesting area of unusual species of pine, fir, cedar, spruce and other, mainly conifer, species. Many of them are seeding freely and you will see a dense mass of young trees, which is regenerating naturally over much of the area.

11. The King's Forest and West Stow Country Park

Grid reference for start TL800715   *Distance 6 miles*

This walk starts and finishes in the car park of the West Stow Country Park. The Park is reached from the B1106 Elveden to Bury St Edmunds road by turning right off this road onto a small lane signed West Stow at the point where the main road turns sharp left about a mile after you leave of the King's Forest. Alternatively, travelling along the A1101 from Barton Mills to Bury St Edmunds, take the turning left, again signed West Stow, about a mile after you pass through the village of Icklingham. In either case follow the brown tourist signs to the Country Park.

There are toilets, a cafeteria and a shop at the Country Park Visitor Centre, which is owned and operated by St Edmundsbury Borough Council. The Park is open from 9.00 am to 8.00 pm in the summer and 9.00 am to 5.00 pm in the winter. Gates open one hour later at weekends. (Correct in 2004).

The Walk

From the Visitor Centre take the signed route to the River Lark, along a wide grass track between fences with the reconstructed Anglo-Saxon village away to your right. At the bottom of the slope turn right and then left through trees to reach the river. Turn left to follow the Lark Valley Path, which runs eastwards along the riverbank towards Bury St Edmunds. This is a well-signed way-marked path throughout its length and is easily followed. Just before you reach the remains of an old lock on the river, the Lark Valley Path diverts away from the river and climbs on to drier ground. It then passes behind the old pump house of a disused sewage works before entering the pinewoods of The King's Forest. Follow the way-marked path as it loops through the trees until eventually it leads back onto the bank of the River Lark with superb views over a series of lakes.

After about a mile of sometimes muddy, riverside walking, the path emerges onto a lane where you turn left. Keep to the lane, ignoring a side road to the right, and then at a T-junction turn left. Shortly after this the Lark Valley Path leaves the lane on the right, opposite the entrance to West Stow church, but you need to carry on ahead until, reaching another junction, you turn left again.

Follow this lane for half a mile coming into the tiny village of

West Stow and as you reach the last of the houses on your right, look for a tarmac road on the right, which you follow with forest on the left, and farmland on the right.

This road leads into the King's Forest after about half a mile and the road becomes a stony forest road. Keep straight ahead, passing a house, sheds and buildings on your right and take the first forest road on your left shortly after.

This is a long stretch of forest road that undulates through a variety of trees, some old some young, until after about a mile and a half you reach another track that crosses in front of you. This is the Icknield Way Path and you turn left to descend gently to the public road below. The Path goes straight across and you follow this through a muddy, wooded stretch. If you take the signed Lark Valley Path left through the gate the trail leads back to the Visitor Centre across West Stow Heath. However, I suggest you continue down the muddy track until you arrive at a short stretch of redundant road beside a lake. Climb the stile and turn right onto the path that runs between the lake and the River Lark on your right, until you arrive back at the Visitor Centre where you started the walk.

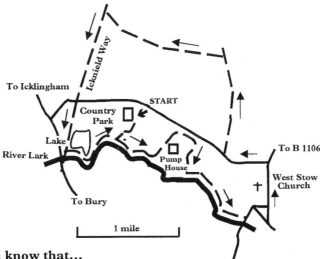

Did you know that...

The 125 acre **West Stow Country Park** is owned and operated by St Edmundsbury Borough Council and is well worth a visit. The Visitor Centre, which was built in 1988, is housed in a large modern building with an excellent shop where you can buy souvenirs and refreshments.

Nearby is the reconstructed **Anglo-Saxon village of West Stow** where a number of huts and other buildings have been built using timber, clay and other natural materials to designs based on archaeological finds in the area.

The **Lark Valley Path** is a way-marked path linking Bury St Edmunds to Mildenhall and following the route of the tiny River Lark, along whose banks it passes for much of the route. The River Lark navigation was created by Act of Parliament in 1700, which allowed for the Lark to be made navigable by boat between Mildenhall and Fornham, near Bury St Edmunds. It was a navigation well into the 19th century with small, shallow draught, horse-drawn boats bringing goods in and out of the area. These included gravel being exported from local gravel workings and coal imported as fuel for the pumping station of the nearby sewage works. The pump house of the old sewage works was built in 1886 and is still standing in the Country Park. The remains of locks can also still be seen where the Lark skirts the Country Park. The river also passes amongst a number of large lakes created by the flooding of pits when gravel extraction was completed. This walk uses a path around the perimeter of one of the lakes and is a favourite spot for anglers and bird-watchers.

The **church of St Mary, West Stow,** lies just off the route of the walk. Largely 15th century, it was derelict by the 19th century and was much restored to its present condition in Victorian times.

There are four species of **deer in Thetford Forest Park** and it is possible to see all four in this area. The most likely to be spotted are the tiny muntjac deer, natives of south-east Asia and escapees from a number of estate parks early in the last century. You also stand a good chance of seeing roe deer and the much larger fallow deer. Largest of all are the native red deer and you may be lucky enough to see one, especially in the autumn and winter. Chinese water deer have been seen elsewhere in the Lark Valley; these secretive cousins of the muntjac favour wet reedy areas along river valleys. The best time to see any of these deer is early morning or late evening.

Roe deer, Muntjac, Fallow deer and Red deer

41

12. Mundford, Lynford Arboretum and Zig-Zag Covert

Grid reference for start TL 805937　　　*Distance 3 miles*

Mundford village is situated where the A134 road from Thetford meets the A1065 from Brandon at a roundabout.

Start this walk in the village itself where there is usually plenty of room to park in the vicinity of the small green in front of the Crown Hotel. The three-mile walk is on good paths and tracks along its entire length and is easily followed.

You can get food and drink in the village and the Crown Hotel and Lynford Hall also serve bar meals and drinks at the usual times. Lynford Hall also boasts a fine restaurant in splendid surroundings.

The Walk

Start the walk from the green and the Crown Hotel taking the road away from the green to the left of the Hotel. The road turns sharply left and right soon after the start and care is needed in case of traffic. Once round the second corner, walk straight ahead towards the main road. Cross the road carefully and take the lane opposite signed for Lynford Hall and the Arboretum. Walk straight ahead up this lane, leaving houses behind and passing double white gates, which are one of the entrances to Lynford Hall.

After about half a mile the road passes the main entrance to Lynford Hall and soon brings you to the Arboretum. The entrance is on your right, opposite the clearly signed car park, which would also make an alternative start to this walk if you wished.

Turn right into the Arboretum and feel free to make your way on any route you choose through this beautiful collection of trees. As long as you walk over the gentle hill through the Arboretum and descend to the lake in the valley below you will not get lost on this walk. When you reach the lake turn left, following the surfaced path to the head of the lake where you cross the two small feeder streams over brick-built bridges.

Once over the bridges, take the grass path straight ahead with a field on your right and a pine plantation on your left. At the end of the path turn right around the corner of the field, to walk along a stoned forest road for a short distance.

You will now have reached the car park at Zig-Zag Covert, which would make another alternative starting point for this particular walk.

Ignore the grass path on the right beside the big notice board and instead go straight ahead on the gravelled path, which then turns right into the big trees of the Covert. The path passes over a small bridge over a flint walled 'folly' and heads into the trees. This is a surfaced path suitable for wheel-chair users and passes a short length of brick wall on the left and the remains of the pool of a fountain on the right.

Bear left along the surfaced path as it winds its way through the Covert before emerging at the end of another lake. Turn left on to a grassy path and left again under the trees at the end of the lake. Then bear right to take the path beside the fenced garden of a cottage to your left.

Follow this path straight ahead, emerging out of the forest, with fields first on your right and then on your left, to reach the main road. Cross the road and then take the narrow lane in front of you, which takes you between houses to the start of your walk.

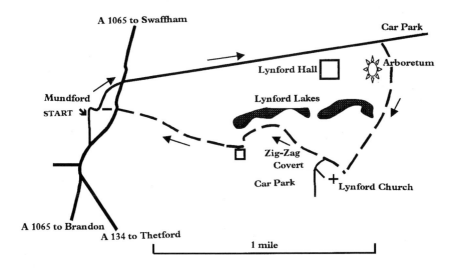

Did you know that...

The present **Lynford Hall** was built in the period 1857-62 replacing an earlier hall built in the early 18th century, which was destroyed by fire. It is a Grade II listed building in the Jacobean style and passed into the hands of the Forestry Commission when they purchased the estate in 1924. It was used as a Forester Training School though this was closed in the 1950s. The original formal garden was constructed in the mid 19th century.

43

The adjoining **Lynford Arboretum** is a splendid collection of trees and there are surfaced paths throughout, making it easy to visit for all ages and abilities. In the spring it is a mass of daffodils, snowdrops and bluebells. Many of the trees were planted by students from the Forestry School in their spare time.

Zig-Zag Covert was where the pleasure gardens of the original Lynford Hall were situated. Within are remnants of the old gardens and some of the features such as statue bases, fountain pools, the brick wall and a short length of flint-walled tunnel.

The tiny Catholic Church of **Our Lady of Consolation and Saint Stephen** can be visited by taking a short diversion at the point where you meet the gravelled path leading into Zig-Zag Covert near the big notice board. If you turn left here and head off down the main forest road, after about 30 yards you will see a narrow driveway on the left through the trees. This is the entrance road to the church, which was built in 1879 at the expense of Mrs Lyne-Stephens of Lynford Hall. The building utilises medieval stone recovered from the demolished church of Saint Helen, now lost in the Covert.

Please respect the privacy of the private house next to the church. Return to the notice board and pick up the route of the walk again.

Mundford village contains many older houses, some of which are built of chalk lump or flint and have thatched roofs. It is a thriving village with several shops, post office, pub and school. The Crown Hotel dates from around 1650.

13. Hockham Woods and The Peddars Way

Grid reference for start TL938919   *Distance 8 miles*

This walk starts from the Forestry Commission car park and picnic site one mile south-west of Hockham Village on the A1075 Thetford to Watton road. It is easy to find as it is clearly signposted. The Eagle pub in nearby Hockham can provide drinks at appropriate times. Be warned that parts of this walk can be wet underfoot at certain times of the year, but don't let this put you off as the walk has much of interest to show you. Most of the route follows public rights of way or permissive paths.

The Walk

From the car park walk away from the main road and take the wide path that leads into the forest. After about a quarter of a mile turn right onto the signed public right of way and shortly after fork right and continue straight ahead until you pass a pole barrier on reaching a narrow country lane.

Here, turn left and follow the lane, crossing over the route of the dismantled Thetford to Watton railway line, until you reach a junction of tarmac roads. Turn right and you have joined the Peddars Way National Path, which heads northwards towards Holme-next-the-Sea, near Hunstanton.

The tarred road soon forks left towards the Military Training Area but you need to take the right fork where the Peddars Way becomes a stony road, which soon runs along the fenced boundary of the military area.

At the point where the fenced military area starts on your left look for the footpath sign indicating a path through the trees on your right and follow this into the forest. This slightly sunken path, which can be a little muddy in places, is a little difficult to see at first but goes straight ahead for nearly half a mile and then, at the corner of a field, turns sharp right along another wooded path. Keep ahead going gently uphill, ignoring side turnings and passing a large shed on the right. Soon after, you will meet a disused railway track and you should then turn right onto this.

Follow the railway track until, just before you reach a bridge, you climb wooden steps and join a footpath, which returns you to the quiet lane you walked along earlier. Turn left and follow the lane.

This does mean going back along your earlier route, but only for a short distance. The lane is bordered on one side by a row of ancient oak trees.

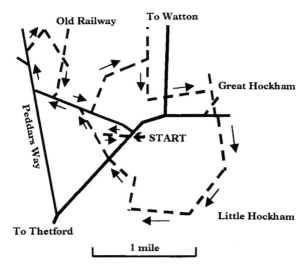

Keep to the lane for about a half a mile and then turn left onto a stony forest road with a steel pole barrier across the entrance. Follow the road, which at first is straight and then bears gently right a couple of times passing round a second pole barrier along the way. After some distance the forest road turns hard left through a third pole barrier and here you turn right onto a grassy track along the edge of a field. At the corner of the field turn left and follow this track, passing a farm on your right to reach a main road.

Carefully cross the main road and continue down Vicarage Lane into the village of Great Hockham. (You could make the village the start of your walk if you wished, as there is usually adequate parking available). Where you reach another road turn right, passing the village green on your left and cross another road heading towards the Eagle pub on the left. Turn left into Harling Road and almost straight away turn right into a very narrow lane called Little Hockham Lane with fields along the left hand side. This lane drops downhill, passing through a wooded section before climbing gently uphill towards a farm at Little Hockham. With a house on the left take a short length of signed footpath along the corner of the field on the right. Then, join a hedged track to the right and strike out between the hedges across the fields towards Hockham Woods.

At the edge of the woods turn right onto a track called Bambridge Lane, which you follow for about three hundred yards. Where the lane bends round a large pit on the right, look for the narrow, signed footpath which forks away between the main entrance to the forest and Bambridge Lane itself, to pass through dense pines. Keep straight ahead on a grassy path ignoring side turnings until you reach a main road.

Cross straight over the main road and walk along this wooded public right of way taking the first turning on your right to return to the car park at the start of the walk.

Did you know that...

The Peddars Way National Trail is nearly 50 miles in length from its starting point on Knettishall Heath in Suffolk to Holme-next-the-Sea near Hunstanton. It is an ancient track way, probably in existence before the Romans, although they modified it and improved it considerably in true Roman fashion. In places the construction of the road, with its cambered surface and shallow drainage gullies either side, (known as the Agger), can still be seen. It is now one of the long-distance national footpaths that criss-cross much of England and connects with the North Norfolk Coast Path, another long-distance path, near Hunstanton. The Way varies from narrow footpath to wide grassy track as you travel its length. You can walk another section of the Peddars Way in Walk 4 in this booklet.

The **Thetford to Watton railway** was constructed in 1869 and was closed to traffic in 1968. It was affectionately known as the 'Crab and Winkle Line' in reference to its sea-food freight. Passenger and goods traffic was carried from Bury St Edmunds to Watton via Thetford and on to Swaffham and King's Lynn. Thetford then had two railway stations and the building for the one that served this line was demolished as recently as 2000.

STANTA (The Stanford Training Area), also known locally as the Battle Area, is the largest single military training area in the East of England. It is an area of some eighteen thousand acres and was acquired by the military authorities in 1942 as a training area for troops in the preparation for the invasion of Europe. The inhabitants of a number of tiny Breckland villages were evacuated to make way for the troops. Today little remains of these hamlets except their churches, which are protected and maintained by the army. Relatives of those evicted are allowed to visit the churches and their attendant graveyards, by arrangement. Apart from this, civilian access is prohibited at all times. Today the area is the largest single stretch of Breckland heath and has considerable conservation value, the wildlife living in apparent harmony with the noisy activities of the soldiers.

The stretch of disused railway line that you walked is part of a circular trail known as **The Great Eastern Pingo Trail**, a permissive path with a car park and starting point further north along the main road to Watton. Pingos are small bodies of water, sometimes, but not always, contained within shallow banks, which were formed during the last Ice Age. As the ice retreated this part of the country was subjected to perma-frost conditions with freezing and expansion of pockets of underground ice in the winter, followed by some thawing in the slightly warmer summer periods. Repeated over hundreds of years this action caused shallow depressions to be formed and when the pockets of ice finally melted these were left and today retain water for much of the year. Indeed, some of the larger pingos hold water permanently. The complex distribution of the pingos has proved of considerable value for water-loving plants, insects and amphibians. You can see examples of pingos in the woodland on either side of the stretch of road running between the second and third pole barriers as described.

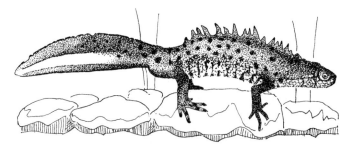

Crested newts may be seen in the pingos

Hockham is a small but interesting village. The pretty village green has a large boulder lying on it. This is a glacial 'erratic', a large boulder transported, perhaps for hundreds of miles, by a glacier at the time of the last Ice Age.

14. Weeting and the Pilgrim's Walk

Grid reference for start TL776893   *Distance 7 miles*

The starting point for this walk is the village of Weeting, which is signposted off the A1065 Brandon to Mundford road. Drive north along Brandon High Street towards the railway station and, immediately after you go over the level crossing, take the left fork which leads towards Weeting. Follow the brown tourist signs for Weeting Castle, which lead you down Church Close to the church of St Mary, and park thoughtfully in the lane close to the church and the castle. The walk is on good paths and tracks throughout. Care is needed at one point on the route to identify an important crossing of tracks. The Saxon pub in the village serves home cooked food and real ales.

The Walk

From your starting point take the lane northwards with the church on your right. The lane leads to a farm and jinks right and left through the farmyard before heading across fields as a track.

Opposite a house take another track on the left. Follow this a short distance until you come to a long, low farm building on the right. Do not take the track on the right immediately alongside this building but instead walk a few more yards before turning right. A straight, sandy path stretches out in front of you initially with a belt of trees on your right. This is the Pilgrim's Walk. Keep to this main path for over a mile as it passes variously through woodland and fields, climbing gently into the forest at a place called Mount Ephraim.

Once inside the main woodland the path climbs a little more steeply to reach a hard forest road at the top. Here, you need to turn right and walk along the forest road. Keep to this road for about half a mile and when it bears hard left continue straight ahead along a grassy path.

Follow this straight grassy track for approximately half a mile ignoring side turnings. The track jinks slightly to the right at a crossing with other tracks and here you need to turn right. *(This crossing of tracks is important to identify, as there are no obvious landmarks on the ground apart from the slight jink in the track).* Keep straight ahead, gently downhill, until you reach another hard forest road. Go straight across this road and after a short

49

distance fork right. Continue steadily downhill on a fairly straight grass track ignoring a turning to the right and one to the left. Eventually a bank of soil will confront you across the path. It is easy to find your way round one side of this bank and out onto a sandy track, which is also a public footpath. Turn left here, and after a short distance you will arrive at the Brandon to Mundford road. Turn right and walk along the very wide grass verge of Emily's Wood picnic area.

At the far end this verge becomes very narrow and you need to take the track that is signed as a footpath through the trees on your right. This track leaves the forest quite quickly and then runs as an avenue of trees with farmland on either side. Pass a farmhouse on your right, keeping straight ahead to the corner of a wood where you turn left along a sandy footpath between fields which, after half a mile, reaches a narrow lane. Go through the gate and turn right along the lane and when it reaches a main road cross straight over and walk along Peppers Close with bungalows on your right. This quiet road bears right, becoming Rectory Lane and then comes out to the main road opposite the bus shelter in the centre of Weeting.

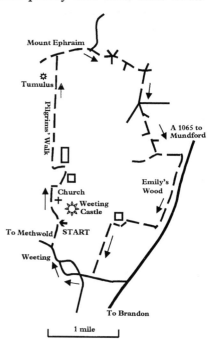

Go straight ahead past the bus shelter and fork right, walking past the school. Continue up the lane to where you parked your car.

Did you know that...

Weeting Castle was built in 1130 on the site of an earlier 10th century settlement. It is a fortified, moated manor house rather than a castle and was abandoned in the 14th century. English Heritage manages it today.

The **church of St Mary** is the village's surviving church. Soon after 1700 the tower of the other church of **All Saints** collapsed on the

nave and destroyed it. Remains of this lost church are still visible in the form of bumps and mounds in the grass in a corner of the recreation ground.

The terrace of thatched cottages opposite the school is known as **The Row**. The cottages date from 1770 and have the longest single-span thatched roof in England.

The Pilgrim's Walk was once part of a pilgrim's route from London and the south to the shrine at Walsingham in north Norfolk. It is sometimes known as the Walsingham Way or Palmer's Way. The latter name is taken from pilgrims who carried palm leaves to show that they had been to the Holy Land. Hidden deep in the forest not far from the Way are the remains of the medieval Walsingham Cross, which today consists of the stump of the stone pillar only.

Legend has it that **Emily's Wood** was the home of a witch named Emily.

Weeting is famous for its **steam and traction engine rally**, which takes place in July each year and has been a feature of village life for more than thirty years. More than 100 steam traction engines gather at the venue, making it one of the largest of its kind to be held in the country. Many of the old steam engines were constructed at the famous Burrell factory in Thetford and you can visit the museum housed in the old paint shop in the town.

15. Two Mile Bottom and Santon Downham

Grid reference for start TL848875   **Distance 5 miles**

Park in the car park at Two Mile Bottom which is on the A134 Thetford to Kings Lynn road about three miles from Thetford town centre. There are attractive picnic facilities at this point as well. There are public toilet facilities at St Helen's picnic site and beside the Forestry Commission Headquarters at Santon Downham, both of which are on the route of this walk.

The Walk

From the car park walk across the grassed area to the main road, which you cross with the greatest care as this is a fast stretch of road, then walk straight ahead down the long, tree-lined forest road. This road is known as Santon Street and was once a route across the heathland to Downham Hall, which was demolished in the mid 1920s.

After about half a mile the road comes into a more open place at a point known as St Helen's Well. This is a grassy mound whose tree-covered slopes drop down to the railway below. At the foot of the mound the Well is a small spring-fed pool of water that trickles away under the railway to the nearby River Little Ouse. Although over-grown it is possible to find a way round the mound to the left and discover the little pool of crystal clear, still water.

Continue straight ahead along the stony forest road that drops gently downhill before climbing to follow a course parallel to the nearby railway. In the days of steam locomotives the grass verge between the road and the railway was a cultivated fire trace, and prevented fires caused by steam engines from spreading into the adjacent forest. Today it has become a valuable grassland habitat rich in flower and insect species and managed by the Forestry Commission to ensure their future.

After a while you will see a pair of cottages beside the railway line. These were once home to staff employed by the railway companies. To your left, a track drops down beside the cottages, taking you under the railway. It then bears right across an open grassy area to join a tarmac lane by the little church of All Saints at St Helen's picnic place. (For more details about the church and picnic place see Walk 2 in this booklet).

52

Walk along the lane, first passing through the grassy areas popular for picnics and family games. Towards the end of the grassy area, turn left and walk across the grass towards the wooden footbridge over the river. Before you reach the bridge turn right and follow the towpath beside the river. In summer this is an especially beautiful stretch of path with dragonflies on the wing and clumps of vivid purple loosestrife beside the river's edge.

When you reach the white, steel bridge that crosses the river climb the steps and turn right along a quiet lane. (If you were to turn left here and walk about a hundred yards you would reach the village shop at Santon Downham and also more public toilet facilities.) Continue your walk along the lane, ignoring the turning on the right and, just before you reach the railway crossing, turn left through a barrier and go down a track with the railway on your right. This track then turns, taking you under the railway, and climbs uphill a short distance to the forest road. At this point the old fire trace is now covered with some of the finest heather in the locality and is a sea of purple in late summer.

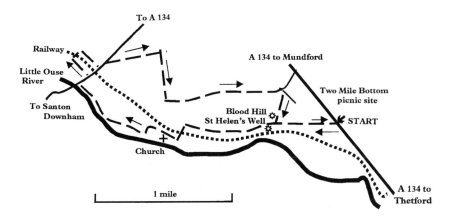

Turn right and walk a short distance along the road to reach the lane again. Here, turn left and almost immediately fork right around a pole barrier to reach another stony forest road that climbs gently uphill.

At the top of the hill turn right and follow the grassy ride to reach another stony road. Here, turn left and follow the road for some distance, ignoring all turnings left or right. The road descends into a dip. Climb up the far slope and, at a point where the stony road bears

53

hard left, turn sharp right onto a grass track between trees. This leads downhill, passing Blood Hill tumulus, to arrive back at Santon Street where, turning left, you walk a short distance back to the start of your walk.

Again, do take care as you cross the main road back into the car park.

Did you know that...

St Helen's Well is located at the foot of a steep cliff beside the railway and close to the Little Ouse. The quarry-like basin that surrounds the Well is the result of quarrying for chalk, which was easily dug and transported by water before the advent of the railway. The spring runs strongly throughout the year and was known as Tenant's Well in the 18th century. High above the pool of water, uneven mounds to the west of the area mark the position of the foundations of the Saxon church known as 'St Helen's Chappell' in 1574.

A track opposite to St Helen's Well on the right hand side of the road leads up to the conspicuous tumulus known as **Blood Hill**. This large mound is of Bronze Age origin and would have been the burial place of an important chieftain at that time. There are many such mounds scattered throughout the forest and across the Breckland area.

The Canadian Army constructed the **white steel bridge**, which crosses the river at Santon Downham, during the First World War, when the area was in extensive use by the military, largely for the storage of munitions in secluded parts of the forest.

Nearby **Santon Downham** village is mentioned in the Domesday Book. (For more information about the village of Santon Downham see Walk 2 in this book.)

16. Harling Woods and Bridgham Village

Grid reference for start TL957858   **Distance 6 miles**

Park carefully in the main street of Bridgham village near to the parish church. To reach the village take the road from Thetford where it leaves the old Norwich Road, signposted Bridgham and Kilverstone, passing the large supermarket and garden centre on your right.

Follow the road, which narrows to become a lane, for about five miles and you will arrive at Bridgham.

The Walk

Walk back towards Thetford for about a quarter of a mile leaving the church on your left, and, where the houses end on the right, take the very small lane on the left, which twists around some narrow bends, and crosses over the pretty River Thet. The lane becomes a sandy track called Bridgham Lane, which climbs gently uphill through trees with houses to right and left.

As the slope levels out, the track widens with a wide grass verge on the right. Keep straight ahead to reach a public road. Cross straight over and follow the track ahead through the trees ignoring any side turnings. The track eventually reaches a quiet, narrow lane; turn hard left onto this lane and follow it for about 200 yards before turning right, round a pole barrier, to walk back into the forest along a wide track through a lovely beech plantation. Keep straight ahead through the trees ignoring side turnings until the track emerges onto a wide grassy ride with a fenced area in front of you. This area is being reverted to heathland and may well have sheep or other stock grazing as part of the management of the grass heath. Turn left and walk along the ride, which is bordered in places by ancient beech, oak and lime trees, some of which are the dead hulks of very old trees. These dead trunks and limbs are valuable habitat for a wide range of invertebrate species and are typical of the ecology of old woodland. This ride is known as 'The Gallops' and was once an impressive tree-lined avenue when in private ownership in the 19th century.

When you reach the end of the fence line, turn right along another grassy track still with the fence line to your right. Keep along the fence until, at the point where there is a small gate on the right, take the track to the left which leads you away from the heathland to emerge on a public road under some lofty beech trees.

Turn right onto this road and within a hundred yards take the turning to the left, signposted 'Harling', which leads along a narrow lane past cottages. Half a mile or so further on, and at the point where the lane bears hard right, turn left away from the road, round a cattle grid and down a stony track.

This next section follows an official public footpath and part of the route is across small arable fields, which may contain crops. Nevertheless the footpath is signed and you are permitted to cross.

You will soon cross a second cattle grid and here, as the main track curves first right and then left, the official footpath is signed on your left through some trees, cutting off the left hand bend of the main track.

The footpath quickly meets this main track again and you cross straight over, climbing a stile to the corner of a small field. The footpath crosses this field, aiming towards a white gate which is at the entrance to the churchyard of the redundant Church of All Saints at West Harling. The church and its tiny graveyard are worth a visit though the church itself is usually locked. The footpath continues in a straight line across another very narrow field coming onto a stony track by the corner of some woodland on your right.

Crossing the stony road the public footpath continues in a straight line crossing the very top corner of a third small field to re-enter the woods.

The whole of the next section should be followed with care, as the path is indistinct in places. Nevertheless, it is a public footpath and is well marked with the characteristic yellow arrows to indicate the route.

Once across the little field after you leave the church, enter the forest through the gap in the trees and follow the path as it winds generally straight ahead. In places additional white arrows have been helpfully painted on trees bordering the route in addition to the official footpath arrows. You will come out of the trees at the rear of the Dower House Caravan Site and the public footpath crosses literally at the rear of the house, before emerging into one of the caravan site fields. Again, the footpath is signed skirting the edge of this field. In a corner you come to a very small building and to the right of this the path re-enters woodland for a short distance following a telephone and electricity line, which are useful guides.

The whole of this next section across farmland follows a public footpath and is well signed.

You leave the narrow stretch of woodland over a stile and out into a field. Cross straight over the field, heading for a stile next to a tree beside a fence. Over the stile turn right and with the fence on your right go through two gates and out into another field this time with the fence on your left. Stay with this fence as it curves gently left over some distance. After a while you come away from the fence following a line of old hawthorn bushes and ancient oak trees. The path descends slightly behind the garden of a house and you need to look hard for a stile partly hidden in bushes. Cross this stile and keep straight ahead and you will soon reach Bridgham Lane over yet another stile. Turn right and retrace your steps downhill along Bridgham Lane and, immediately after crossing the bridge over the River Thet, turn right over a bridge and a stile into a small field. Cross this field diagonally, heading towards a large white-gabled house on the hill in front of you, and so back to the start of your walk.

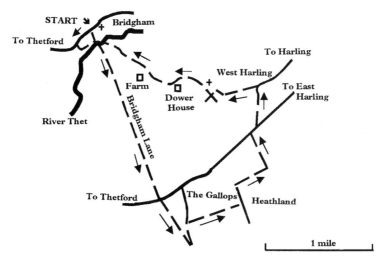

Did you know that...

Bridgham is probably a very old settlement and its name means 'settlement (ham) by a bridge'.

The **church of St Mary the Virgin** in Bridgham is mainly 14th century though records show a church has been here since Saxon times. The wooden bell-turret at the west end of the nave houses a single bell from 1632. A visiting historian recorded 'the steeple down' in 1735 but there are no records to confirm when it fell. Inside, the

57

15th century font is particularly ornate with carved figures around the eight major compass points. It has a 17th century cover.

Bridgham Lane is an old road, where all traffic has right of way. In the past it was a main route into the village as it uses one of the few crossing points of the River Thet in the locality.

The Churches Conservation Trust today manages the **church of All Saints at West Harling**. Although no longer in use for regular worship, it remains a consecrated building, maintained for the benefit of present and future generations. The village of West Harling, which it once served, no longer exists.

The **River Thet** rises north of Snetterton and runs for about 14 miles to join the Little Ouse River in the centre of Thetford town.

The **Dower House Touring Caravan site** is a popular venue for caravan enthusiasts and makes a good base from which to explore the area. It is also the meeting place for local amateur astronomers because it is sited far enough away from habitation to be unaffected by light pollution which can be a problem close to more urban areas.

17. Santon Downham, Grimes Graves and the Harling Drove

Grid reference for start TL 816876   *Distance 6 miles*

This walk starts in the car park at the Forestry Commission offices in Santon Downham. Santon Downham is clearly signposted from the main road between Thetford and Brandon and the offices are well signed once in the village. Please park thoughtfully in this car park as it can be very busy in office hours. There are public toilets in the car park and the adjacent village shop offers friendly service for snacks and soft drinks.

The Walk

Leave the car park, walking downhill between buildings where the road twists through a narrow section. Once through the narrow section the road widens to cross the River Little Ouse by a steel lattice bridge constructed during the First World War by troops from the Canadian army who were stationed in the area.

Continue ahead up the lane, cross the railway crossing and turn sharp right into Santon Street, a forest road running parallel to the railway, which was once the main road between Santon and Thetford. A fence encloses this section of the walk as it is an area being returned to heathland and is grazed by sheep from time to time as part of its management. After about a quarter of a mile the road forks and you should take the left fork, following the road as it climbs uphill ignoring a grassy path to the left. At a cross roads near the brow of the hill turn left along a grassy ride which you follow for another half a mile ignoring any turnings to left or right. You will then come to a steel pole barrier and, on passing round this, turn left onto the Harling Drove.

Almost immediately, go straight across a narrow lane continuing along the sandy route of the Harling Drove. The Drove descends gently, then, after a couple of hundred yards, look for a grassy track which forks right, away from the Drove and staying on the higher ground. Where this meets another grassy track, turn right, uphill, and almost immediately take the right fork near the brow of the hill. This track emerges shortly onto a stony forest road with an area of fenced open ground ahead. Go straight across, climb the stile, and continue downhill to reach another fence. The area you have just walked

59

through is another heathland area which is slowly being restored by grazing, for its wildlife interest. The open grassy area beyond the second fence is full of mysterious hollows and mounds. This is Grimes Graves, the site of Neolithic flint mines owned and managed by English Heritage. There is a visitor centre where you can find out about the history of the place as well as buying souvenirs. You can also purchase a ticket which gives you access, down a ladder, to one of the flint mines some thirty feet below. For details of how to visit this area see the notes at the end of this walk.

Turn left along the grassy track, keeping the fence to your right, and aim for a stile in the corner. Climb over the stile and keep straight ahead for about two hundred yards where you will come out onto the stony forest road beside a corrugated-steel-covered emergency water supply tank used to fight forest fires. Almost straight away, turn right, away from the forest road, and go downhill along a grassy path. At the bottom of the hill turn left and walk gently uphill along the bottom of a shallow valley. Near the top of the hill you come to a cross roads of grassy paths and you need to turn left. Keep to this path ignoring tracks to right and left. The grassy path jinks slightly here and continues straight ahead with tall beech trees on your right before eventually coming out onto the forest road again.

Go straight across the road and through a belt of mainly birch and sweet chestnut trees and then climb gently uphill through dark pines. These are middle-aged trees and will soon start to show their real majesty as they are thinned out in the coming years. After some distance you will come to a T-junction of paths. Turn left here and continue along a straight, grassy path. For most of the way along here you will find very mixed woodland on your right. This is a Research Trial area where many species of trees have been tested over the years. Many of them are seeding freely into the adjoining plan-tations to create a woodland rich in species, variety and age.

Ignoring a turning on your left, keep ahead to the end of this ride where you meet another T-junction. Turn right and soon you come to yet another intersection. Turn right and for a short distance you will be on a section of path you walked in the opposite direction earlier in the walk. This time keep straight downhill and ignore the path on your left.

At the bottom of the hill you will reach the Harling Drove running across in front of you. Cross over the Drove going around yet another pole barrier and within twenty yards you will reach a stony road with the railway beyond. Turn left and follow the road as it runs by the railway track, looking out for a path on your right which drops steeply down to go under the railway. The path bears left on the other side of the tracks and you simply follow it back to the lane which, on turning right, will take you back to Santon Downham and the start of your walk.

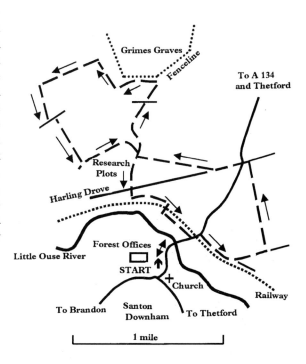

Did you know that...

In 1668 the river near Santon Downham was almost blocked by a **great sandstorm,** which blew huge quantities of sand from the adjacent heaths into the valley, almost swamping the tiny village at the same time. For more information about Santon Downham village see Walk 2 in this book.

The areas of **heathland** are important wildlife conservation areas. Heathland is an internationally endangered habitat and the restoration work is being carried out by Forest Enterprise in partnership with English Nature and local Wildlife Trusts. 'Flying flocks' of sheep are moved from area to area throughout the year and their grazing keeps the grass and heather at a level maintained to give maximum wildlife value. Unlike the heather heaths of the south of England, which are exclusively on acid sandy soils, Breckland heaths tend to be grassy or grass mixed with heather as the soils in this area are less acid and are influenced by the chalk below. They have a flora and fauna unique to the Brecks.

The **Harling Drove** runs from Roudham Heath in the east through to Hockwold-cum-Wilton on the edge of the fens to the west. At one time it originated at East Harling, even further to the east, but that section of the route is untraceable having been largely lost by the construction of the railway and other developments in earlier centuries. It is a historic Drove road developed for the purpose of moving stock and other goods to and from the Fens and the Norfolk hinterland. For much of its distance it runs on sandy paths and tracks through the forest, although after leaving the forest near Weeting it now follows the line of modern roads.

Grimes Graves has a fascinating history. Between three and four thousand years ago Neolithic man sunk deep pits into the ground in search of the highest quality flint known. He used this flint to fashion stone axes, arrowheads, scrapers and other tools for his use. The visitor centre at Grimes Graves explains the history in detail and for a modest entrance charge there is the chance to climb down a ladder to the floor of one of the pits some 30 feet below to view the underground galleries dug by these ancient people in search of one of the most valuable commodities of their time. The entrance to Grimes Graves is via the minor road that leaves the A134 from Thetford at Lynford and then runs through to link to the A1065, Brandon to Mundford road. The site is well signed in the general area with the familiar brown tourist signs. Opening times are 10.00 am to 6.00 pm between April and September, with slightly shorter hours during the rest of the year. It would be wise to check before you visit.

The **water meadows** by the Little Ouse near Santon Downham are rare examples of wetland habitat in the midst of the somewhat arid, sandy expanse of the Brecklands and are renowned for the moisture-loving plants and creatures that abound there. An information board beside the path under the railway line gives plenty of detail about the site.

18. Swaffham Forest and Cockley Cley

Grid reference for start TF767090   ***Distance 9 miles***

The start of this walk is in the Forestry Commission car park in Swaffham Forest. The car park is reached via the A47 Swaffham by-pass and the A1122 Downham Market road. It is signed off the A1122 about half a mile from the roundabout on the A47 and is a short distance down a forest road. It would be possible to start and finish the walk in Cockley Cley village if you preferred, simply picking up the directions for the walk at the appropriate part of the route described.

Most of the walk is on public footpaths, forest roads and quiet lanes and the paths are generally in very good order. This is a very rural part of Norfolk with few amenities on your route. However, the Twenty Church Wardens pub in Cockley Cley, is approximately half way round the walk and you can get good pub food here at appropriate times.

The Walk

From the car park turn left and continue along the hard forest road you arrived on. After a short distance the forest road bears left through a barrier before heading off into the forest. However, the walk goes straight ahead along the public right of way, which continues as a wide track, initially with forest on one side only, and then, after passing a farm on the left, with the forest on both sides.

Keep to this track, ignoring all side turnings, until you reach more farm buildings, this time on your right. Walk past them and then look for the signed bridleway going back on you to the right and into the farmyard. The signed bridleway then goes away from the farm across fields. Eventually the bridleway reaches another at a crossing of tracks by a house. Here turn left and go straight ahead until you reach a junction with lanes. Take the lane straight ahead, signed Cockley Cley, and follow this as it bears left and comes back into woodland. After leaving the wooded area continue ahead for a mile or so keeping to the lane which threads its way through farmland edged with Scots pine trees.

This lane eventually descends into the little village of Cockley Cley with the Twenty Church Wardens pub on the corner. (If you don't want the extra distance into Cockley Cley, look for the bridleway sign on the left turning hard back on your route and start the return leg from there). Once in the village the church, with its fallen tower, is just around the corner from the Twenty Church Wardens. After visiting the village retrace your steps up the lane for about a quarter of a mile.

After you leave the last houses behind, look out for the signed bridleway forking off through trees to your right. Leaving the trees, the path drops gently downhill beside a field and a barn on the left and then climbs gently up towards the forest. As you reach the edge of the forest the bridleway is signed away to the left, initially with a field on the left, before entering the woodland proper. Here it goes straight ahead on a well-signed path until, reaching farmland; it turns right and follows the edge of the forest gently uphill.

At the top of the hill the path faces a fenced compound with sheds and you turn left along a short stretch of track with concrete strips for vehicles to run on, to reach another lane near Drymere.

Turn right onto the quiet lane and follow it through the hamlet of Drymere for about three quarters of a mile. At the end of a field on the left, after you leave houses behind, look for the entrance to the forest beside the field, with a barrier set well back off the road. Follow this hard forest road as it passes through the forest for about two miles. The road follows a fairly straight course and you should ignore all side turnings. Eventually the road drops into a dip and passes through a double barrier. It then climbs a steep section, bears hard left and comes to yet another barrier. Go round this and bear right to arrive back at the road leading from the car park at the start of the walk.

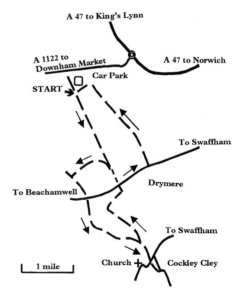

64

Did you know that...

In **Cockley Cley** village there is a reconstruction of an Iceni village. Queen Boudicca (Boadicea) was queen of the Iceni tribe, which was powerful in East Anglia around 2,000 years ago. The reconstructed village is open to the public from April to October and is a splendid day out for families. Nearby are the ruins of the Saxon church of Saint Mary dating from c 628 AD.

The **church of All Saints, Cockley Cley** was restored in 1866. On 29 August 1991 the tower collapsed. This has been the fate of a number of similar church towers of flint and chalk construction in the Brecks over the years.

The **Twenty Church Wardens** pub has only been a public house since 1968. It was converted from a former schoolhouse, which closed in 1930, to serve as a meeting place for residents. It is now a popular country pub serving good food and beers at appropriate times.

Swaffham is an interesting small town nearby. It is full of old buildings of interest and still holds weekly markets. The town sign features the story of the **Pedlar of Swaffham**. This was a man who went to London and, on the point of throwing himself off London Bridge, was dissuaded from doing so by a stranger. He then had a dream that there was buried treasure in a far off place, which he recognised as being his own garden. Without more ado he returned to Swaffham and from his garden dug up two pots of gold!

Swaffham Raceways is a local car-racing circuit, featuring stock-car racing. It is also a greyhound-racing stadium. It can be found near the roundabout on the A47 where you take the Downham Market road to get to the start of this walk.

At the point where you reach the lane in **Drymere** village you are at one of the highest points in this part of Norfolk with good views of the surrounding countryside. The large, grey, concrete pillar standing beside the road here is a **trig point**, used by the Ordnance Survey for many years when they surveyed the area. Map-makers were able to take compass bearings and elevations from this point to other trig points or buildings such as churches to help them build up their maps. Sadly, such points are now redundant, more accurate mapping being possible using satellite technology and Global Positioning Systems (GPS).

In the front garden of a house on the left, as you walk through Drymere, is a large boulder. This is an **'erratic'**, a large boulder brought from hundreds of miles away and dumped here by a retreating ice sheet at the end of the last Ice Age.

19. A Short Walk in Mildenhall Woods

Grid reference for start TL739741   *Distance 2 miles*

This short walk starts from the entrance into the forest beside the A1101 Mildenhall to Bury St Edmunds road. From the Five-Ways roundabout at Barton Mills on the A11 take the Bury St Edmunds road and look for the entrance into the woods numbered 306 on your left, about three quarters of a mile from the roundabout. Please park so that the entrance is not blocked as it is in daily use for forest work to take place.

The Walk

Go round the barrier and walk straight ahead up the hill on the forest road. After about 200 metres the stoned road ends with sandy tracks going ahead and to right and left. Take the track to the left, which descends gently through the trees, and then take the first turning on the right beside a small clearing in the trees. This track leads you to another clearing with a fenced area to one side. This is a nature reserve where the rare military orchid is protected.

Immediately opposite the corner of the fence, look for a faint track to the right, going through the pines and firs. This track is rather indistinct but as long as you go forward through the trees you will reach a more obvious track going ahead up the hill after no more than fifty yards. Follow this, climbing uphill and running parallel with the A11 road whose traffic you cannot fail to hear. The track goes over the brow of the hill and descends steadily for about a mile. At the bottom of the hill the forest ends beside farmland and you should turn right and follow the track along the forest boundary.

After a while you will reach a fenced area and you turn right, keeping the fence line on your left. After a little while you reach a gate and stile that you can cross over to continue ahead on a sandy track, now within the fenced area. (During the bird-nesting season you may find notices requesting you do not enter the fenced area, in which case simply continue to follow the path along the fence line). Please be aware that sheep or cattle may be grazing this area and it is more important than ever that you keep dogs on a lead if they are accompanying you on the walk.

Simply follow this track over the hill with superb views of neighbouring heathland to your left the whole way. When you reach the second fence go through the gate, turn left and descend to where you parked your car.

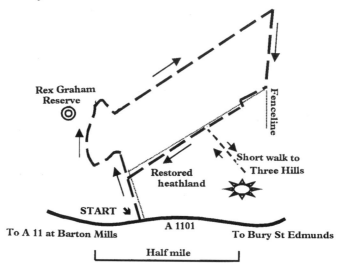

Rex Graham Reserve

Fenceline

Short walk to Three Hills

Restored heathland

START

To A 11 at Barton Mills

A 1101

To Bury St Edmunds

Half mile

Did you know that...

The small fenced area protecting the scarce orchid is the **Rex Graham Reserve.** It is a Site of Special Scientific Interest (SSSI) as this is one of the few sites in the country where the military orchid grows. The site is open to visitors one weekend each spring when the orchids are in flower.

The large fenced area is being reverted from forest to **heathland** as part of a programme of restoration of valuable heathland sites being undertaken by Forest Enterprise in association with local Wildlife Trusts and English Nature. Grazing with sheep or cattle is the main means of achieving the required intensity of vegetation and thus allowing important heathland plants to flourish. The panoramic view over the nearby National Nature Reserves of **Tuddenham and Cavenham heaths** gives an idea of how extensive heathland once was in this part of East Anglia.

Within the fenced area you may make a short diversion by following the path off to the left about halfway up the hill. This leads to a curious area of broken ground with deep valleys and hummocks over a wide area. This is **Three Hills** and it is a Site of Special Scientific

Interest for its archaeological, geological and botanical interest. The archaeological interest is that this was an Anglo-Saxon burial ground. Geologically, the steep ridge, broken by a number of old gravel workings, represents the bank of an ancient river that once flowed eastwards to join the Rhine in what is now the North Sea. Botanically, the whole area is rich in rare and unusual plants peculiar to the Breckland heaths. Rare heathland birds such as the **stone curlew, woodlark and nightjar** also favour the site and during the nesting season you may find notices asking you to keep out of the fenced area to avoid disturbance to the birds and their young.

You will need to retrace your steps to rejoin the main route and continue the walk.

20. The Thetford Chase Walk

Grid reference for start TL796835   *Distance 12 miles*

I have included this walk because it gives you the opportunity, once a year, to do a particularly long walk and at the same time participate in a mass walk where people of all ages are encouraged to raise money for charity by sponsorship.

The event started in 1969 and was originally along a single route from West Stow to High Ash with a coach shuttle service to take walkers back to their cars. It now consists of a circular walk entirely within the forest. It has taken place every year since 1969 except in 2001 when the foot-and-mouth outbreak curtailed countryside access.

Organised by Suffolk County Council with assistance from Forest Enterprise, RAYNET and St John Ambulance, the walk takes place on a Saturday, usually in March or April. It starts at Mayday field, which is about 2 miles south east of Brandon on the B1106 Elveden road. It is always very well signposted and is easily found.

Often up to a thousand walkers take part in this 12-mile, well-signed, circular walk around the forest. Most are young people and members of youth groups, colleges and schools, but individuals are encouraged to take part if they wish, no matter what their age. Walkers seek sponsorship for any charity they wish and the reward is a fine medal for completing the walk and, hopefully, a valuable donation to their favourite charity.

Details can be obtained in the early spring each year by contacting either the local Forest Office at Santon Downham on 01842 810271, which will put you in touch with the organisers, or by contacting them direct on 01638 663740. (Information correct as at 2004).

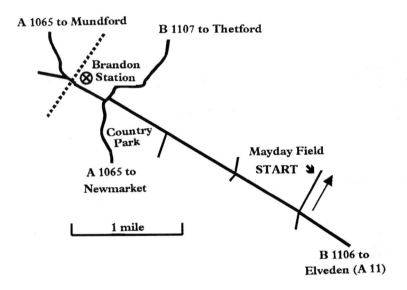